Economic and Social Commission for Asia and the Pacific

URBAN GEOLOGY AND THE IMPACT ON OUR LIVES

Samples from daily life in Bangkok

ATLAS OF URBAN GEOLOGY
Volume 13

United Nations
New York, 2001

ST/ESCAP/2180

UNITED NATIONS PUBLICATION
Sales No. E.02.II.F.32
Copyright © United Nations 2001
ISBN: 92-1-120094-6

The designations employed and the presentation of the material in this publication do not imply the expression of any opinion whatsoever on the part of the Secretariat of the United Nations concerning the legal status of any country, territory, city or area or of its authorities, or concerning the delimitation of its frontiers or boundaries.

The opinions, figures and estimates set forth in this publication are the responsibility of the authors, and should not necessarily be considered as reflecting the views or carrying the endorsement of the United Nations.

Mention of firm names and commercial products does not imply the endorsement of the United Nations.

This publication has been issued without formal editing.

FOREWORD

The Atlas of Urban Geology series is published by ESCAP in an effort to familiarize member countries with the outcome of a series of projects that are aimed at inducing central and local governments to make more efficient use of their own in-house expertise in earth sciences such as exists in national geological survey departments. Doing so should enhance the chances of attaining sustainable urban development, a professed goal of virtually all governments in the Asia-Pacific region, where soon city dwellers will outnumber rural populations.

Sustainability is a problem anywhere, but cities with a population of more than a million are especially hard put to stave off the ill effects of natural hazards and environmental degradation, both of which have negative impacts on people's livelihoods. The United Nations Centre for Human Settlements (Habitat) counts 326 of such megacities worldwide; soon most of them will be in the ESCAP region. Little wonder then, that the 21st century has been labeled the "City Century" by Habitat, while the United Nations General Assembly even went as far as using the term "Urban Millenium". The UN Secretary General, Mr. Kofi Annan pointed out that two thirds of large cities in developing countries lack proper sewerage systems, while domestic garbage is being dumped in unsuitable waste disposal sites. To properly address both issues, the advice of geological institutions is indispensible. This message is increasingly being heard and understood, with more and more member countries considering geological conditions as part of their planning and decision-making.

Growing public awareness is often an important factor in such an official change in environmental policy. The two papers in this volume both contain elements of public concern, and are therefore expected to reach a wider readership.

The secretariat is thankful for the continued support by the Government of the Netherlands for the above-mentioned successive projects, the latest of which bearing the self-explanatory title "Using knowledge of surface and underground conditions of land resources to improve and support urban planning and development". Interested readers are invited to let us have their comments and/or feedback via the ESCAP website www.unescap.org and subsidiary homepages.

The secretariat

geol
QE
39.5
.U7
U63
2001g

CONTENTS

Page

I. THE IMPACT OF URBAN GEOLOGY ON OUR LIVES

Summary		1
A.	Introduction	1
B.	Geology for planning – urban geoscience	2
	1. Geology for planning data	3
	2. Urban geology and ESCAP	4
C.	Urban expansion, geological management	5
D.	Urban geology and you	5
	1. Transport of solid materials to the city	6
	2. Urbanization and soils	8
	3. Urban soil management	9
	4. Urban water management	10
	(i) *Groundwater characteristics*	11
	(ii) *Subsidence*	13
E.	Bangkok urban geological data	14
	1. Bangkok coastal location – a historical perspective	14
	2. Bangkok geology	16
	3. Pumping impact	18
	4. Groundwater management discussion	19
F.	Hazards	23
	1. Introduction	23
	2. Bangkok assessment	23
	(i) *Earthquakes*	23
	(ii) *Flooding and storms*	25
	(iii) *Sea level rise and basin subsidence*	26
G.	Natural stone in cities	26
H.	Urban geology, costs and benefits	28
J.	Managing data or saving money	29
References		31

II. LAND SUBSIDENCE IN BANGKOK: AN OVERVIEW OF CHANGES DURING THE LAST 23 YEARS

A.	Introduction	33
	1. Land subsidence	33
	2. Previous research in the Bangkok area	33
	3. Research project	34
	4. Internship programme	34
	5. Acknowledgements	35
B.	Description of the project area	35
	1. Geology and hydrogeology of the Central Plain	35
	(i) *General geologic setting*	35
	(ii) *The Bangkok Clay*	37
	(iii) *Spatial variation in thickness of the Bangkok Clay*	39

CONTENTS *(continued)*

Page

    2. Climate, water levels and tide 41
        (i)   Climate of the Central Plain 41
        (ii)   Chao Phraya River 41
        (iii) Tide and sea level in the Gulf of Thailand 42
    3. Anthropogenic factors 42
        (i)   Growth of Bangkok 42
        (ii)   Canals in Bangkok 43
    4. Water use in the Central Plain 43
        (i)   Total water use and water supply in the Central Plain 43
        (ii)   Legal and organizational aspects of groundwater use 44
        (iii) Amount of groundwater pumpage 44
        (iv) Hydrologic aspects of groundwater pumpage 45
    5. Historical overview of the situation in Bangkok 46

C.   Land subsidence 47
    1. Introduction 47
    2. Causes and geotechnical processes 47
        (i)   Land subsidence mechanisms 47
        (ii)   Geotechnical methods used to calculate land subsidence 48
        (iii) Causes of land subsidence in the Central Plain 50
    3. Techniques of measuring land subsidence and available data 51
        (i)   General techniques to measure land subsidence 51
        (ii)   Data sources used in this study 52
    4. Maps showing land subsidence in the Bangkok area 54
        (i)   Methodology to create the maps 54
        (ii)   Land subsidence maps: single years 55
        (iii) Land subsidence maps: three-year periods 58
        (iv) Land subsidence maps: whole period 66

D.   Consequences of land subsidence and the overpumping of groundwater 68
    1. Introduction 68
    2. Prolonged and extended flooding 68
        (i)   General 68
        (ii)   Flooding and health 69
        (iii) Tidal floods 69
    3. Damage to the infrastructure 70
        (i)   Breakage of sewers and pipelines 70
        (ii)   Damage to roads and bridges 72
        (iii) Well head protrusion 73
    4. Deterioration of the natural drainage system 73
    5. Intrusion of saline water 74
        (i)   General 74
        (ii)   Dispersion 74

CONTENTS (continued)

Page

	6.	Coastal erosion	75
		(i) Land subsidence compared with sea level rise	75
		(ii) Coastal erosion	75
E.	Conclusions and recommendations		77
	1.	Conclusions	77
		(i) Land subsidence and groundwater management	78
		(ii) Predictions for future land subsidence	78
	2.	Expectations for future consequences	78
	3.	Suggestions for action	79
		(i) Suggested remedial measures	79
		(ii) Need for action to come to a better scientific understanding	79
References			80

List of tables

No.		Page
I.1.	Estimated annual consumption of mineral commodities by a city of 250,000 people	6
I.2.	Proportion of total city area occupied by open space and proportion of the open area regarded as green space	9
I.3.	Urban population with access to water supply and sanitation	12
II.1.	Description of the Bangkok multi aquifer system	38
II.2.	Rainfall characteristics	41
II.3.	Chronology of events, researches and remedial measures taken to curb land subsidence	47
II.4.	Compression indices for tested deltaic facies in the Mississippi Delta	50
II.5.	Overview of general Compression Index Values for clays in the Central Plain	50
II.6.	Schematic overview in methods used to measure land subsidence	52
II.7.	Data sources of land subsidence data in the Central Plain	52
II.8.	Number of dates and surveys of AIT stations	53
II.9.	Surveys carried out over the MGL-project datapoints, and the number and percentage leveled in the respective studies	54
II.10.	Overview of periods used to show land subsidence	58

CONTENTS *(continued)*

Page

List of figures

No.

I.1.	Degree of urbanization	2
I.2.	Heavy trucks transporting rocks or sand to the city cause dust, pollution and road damage	7
I.3.	Large-scale extraction of construction materials to build the city leads to local environmental degradation without proper controls	8
I.4.	Discharge of a modern sewerage plant	11
I.5.	Cracking of the road surface around installed drainage inlets	13
I.6.	Bangkok, the sinking city	14
I.7.	Subsidence: original surface was at the bottom of the door	15
I.8.	Dike to protect mangrove forest, Bangkok shoreline	15
I.9.	Looking across eroded shoreline, with local transgression of 5 m/annum. Protected land in the background	16
I.10.	Growth of Bangkok	17
I.11.	Reshaped oxbow lake, an old meander of the Chao Phraya River	18
I.12.	Schematic stratigraphic section underlying Bangkok	19
I.13.	Cracks appear at the foot of buildings due to subsidence and compaction of the top layers	20
I.14.	Cracks appearing at bridge/road linkages, as bridges stand on piles while roads are built on shrinking subsoil	21
I.15.	Groundwater level rise in the Chalk aquifer beneath London (1970-1995)	22
I.16.	Building up roads to compensate for subsidence causes elevation problems at crossings	22
I.17.	Rebuilt road, about 50 cm higher than adjacent land, causing flooding problems during the rainy season	23
I.18.	Reconstruction of the region at 20 Ma. Rotation of Borneo and parts of Malaya, Sumatra and Java began. Subduction of the proto-South China Sea caused a split of the Sula arc and the separation of the active arc of the Cagayan ridge. The opening of the South China Sea propagated in a south-westerly direction onto the Sunda shelf	24
I.19.	Reconstruction of the region at 15 Ma. Rotation of Borneo and parts of Malaya, Sumatra and Java were under way. Strike-slip motion at the southern boundary of the Philippine Sea plate fragmented the Bird's Head microcontinent and moved blocks west in the plate boundary zone. Similar motions were occurring in the northern Philippines. The back-arc Sulu Sea began to close after collision of the Cagayan ridge with the Palawan margin	25
I.20.	Reconstruction of the region at 10 Ma. Between 5-25 Ma the Philippine Sea plate rotated about a pole at 15°N, 160°E. Counterclockwise rotation of Borneo and related rotations of Sundaland were complete	26
I.21.	Example of granite pavement properly selected and installed	27
I.22.	Granite cracking due to poor installation and specifications of the selected stone	27
II.1.	Map of the structural basin of the Central Plain. The faults, depth of the Quaternary sediments, locations of some deep drillings and the main topographic features are represented on this map	36

CONTENTS *(continued)*

Page

II.2.	Hydrogeologic north-south profile of the lower Central Plain showing the principal aquifers of the Bangkok Multi Aquifer System	37
II.3.	Map of the Lower Central Plain showing the extension and thickness of the Holocene Soft Clay. Locations of the corings are also shown	40
II.4.	Map with the thickness of the Bangkok Clay	40
II.5.	Expansion of Bangkok over the years.	42
II.6.	Groundwater pumpage in the Bangkok area since 1955, in millions of cubic metres per day (CMD, vertical axis); on the horizontal axis the year as, top: BE, below: AD	45
II.7.	Sketch showing groundwater pumping and flow response from a multi-aquifer/aquitard system	49
II.8.	Location of the AIT and DMR datapoints in the project area.	55
II.9.	Land subsidence in the year 2000	56
II.10.	Land subsidence in the year 1979	57
II.11.	Rate of land subsidence in the period 1978-1981	59
II.12.	Rate of land subsidence in the period 1981-1985	60
II.13.	Rate of land subsidence in the period 1985-1988	61
II.14.	Rate of land subsidence in the period 1988-1991	62
II.15.	Rate of land subsidence in the period 1991-1994	63
II.16.	Rate of land subsidence in the period 1994-1997	64
II.17.	Rate of land subsidence in the period 1997-2000	65
II.18.	Total land subsidence between 1978 and 2000	66
II.19.	Total land subsidence between 1992 and 2000	67
II.20.	Tidal flood in Phra Pradaeng, near the Chao Phraya River mouth	70
II.21.	Land subsidence at the Huay Kwai Waste Water Treatment Plant. The surface was originally connected to the building. Since the building is on piles resting on the bearing sand layer, and the road is not, the latter subsided	71
II.22.	Land subsidence at the Huay Kwai WWTP. The end of the drainpipe must have been only slightly above the ground surface. Its end is now about 70 cm above the ground. The arrow indicates the former ground level	71
II.23.	Damage to a bridge in the old town of Bangkok (Charoen Krung Road); extra steps are necessary for pedestrians to enter the bridge	72
II.24.	Damage to a pavement in Bang Kapi. Note the differences in height between the unfounded road and the founded building	72
II.25.	A land subsidence bowl has developed in Eastern Bangkok. The deepest point of the bowl is just below 0 m and is therefore more than 1 metre lower than the surrounding area	73
II.26.	Principle of saline groundwater intrusion in an aquifer	74
II.27.	Geodetic levellings reveal a lowering of the land of more than 60 cm at AIT benchmark No. 24 (at the coast in Samut Prakan, near the Chao Phraya River mouth between 1978 and 1996)	76
II.28.	Coastal erosion and disappearance of mangrove coast near the mouth of the Ta Chin River, Samut Sakhon Province	76

LIST OF ABBREVIATIONS

AD	Anno Domini
AIT	Asian Institute of Technology
BE	Buddhist Era (as used in Thai Calendar)
BMA	Bangkok Metropolitan Administration
BP	(years) Before Present
CMD	Cubic metres per day
DMR	Department of Mineral Resources
ESCAP	Economic and Social Commission for Asia and the Pacific
IPCC	Intergovernmental Panel on Climate Change
JICA	Japan International Cooperation Agency
ka	thousand years
M	million
MGL	Mitigation of Groundwater crisis and Land subsidence (in the Bangkok area – a DMR project)
MSL	Mean Sea Level
MWA	Metropolitan Waterworks Authority
NEDECO	Netherlands Engineering Consultants
PWA	Provincial Waterworks Authority
RTSD	Royal Thai Survey Department
UN	United Nations

I. THE IMPACT OF URBAN GEOLOGY ON OUR LIVES

by

F.H. Ariesen[1]

Summary

Knowledge of geology has been used throughout our history to decide on locating human settlements. The rapid development of science and cities over the last century made the influence of geology on our daily life appear less obvious, and geological know-how developed into a search for commodities and overall under-standing of our planet.

Cities are totally dependent on their geological setting. Failing to take geological conditions into account causes many problems. Subsoil conditions control the necessity for piling, groundwater availability, sewerage disposal, and drainage, soil conditions are important when deciding where to build, create parks, etc., while regional geological parameters control the hazards which may affect a human settlement.

The complex nature of understanding in detail the geological conditions, engineering possibilities, the need for infrastructure development, groundwater and sewerage management, transport requirements as well as financial parameters require the close cooperation of people from various parts of the society to integrate all this information, so that proper decisions can be made. Geology for planning and in particular "urban geology" aims at promoting such an approach.

This paper describes the main geological elements effecting urbanization, with examples mainly from Bangkok, showing what happens every day. Each part may appear small but as the effects are cumulative, the ultimate overall outcome is staggering. Understanding, controlling and applying urban geology allows huge savings not only in monetary terms, but also in preventing misery to the city's inhabitants.

The aim of this paper is to show to the impact of geology on our daily life in the city, without getting too involved in scientific detail. This approach offers the opportunity to all people interested in proper city management to familiarize themselves with the most common pitfalls and problems that may occur.

The introduction of the urban geology into the Asian and Pacific region has been promoted keenly by ESCAP since 1988 and about US $500,000 has hitherto been spent as seed money in this effort. Several member countries have responded well to this initiative and started their own national services. Huge cost savings have already been realized by following this scientific approach. Nonetheless, further development and promotion is needed to spread awareness throughout ESCAP membership.

A. Introduction

In the last half century a dramatic change in lifestyle took place. Until the end of the Second World War only a minority of the world population lived in an urbanized environment, whereas now this amounts to about 50 per cent (see figure I.1). The fastest growth occurs in South Asia and Africa.

---

[1] Geologist and Director, Hin Saeng Nakorn Co., Ltd., #13-35 T1 Building, Muang Thong Thani 3, Chaeng Wattana Road, Pakkred, Nontha Buri 11120, Thailand.

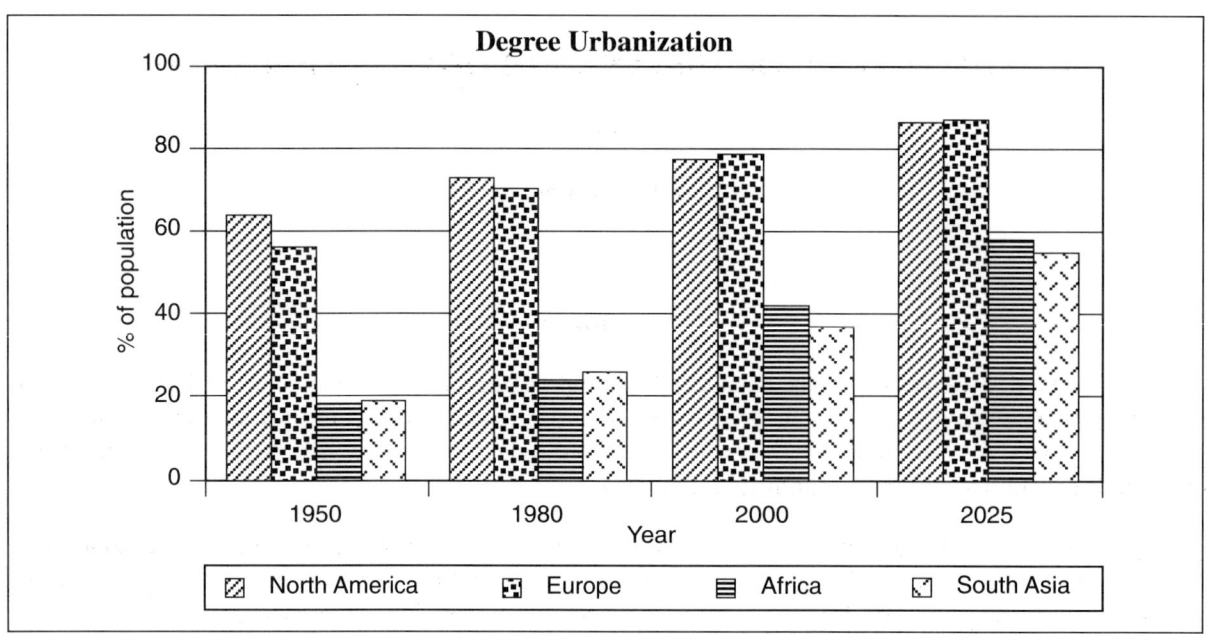

Figure I.1. Degree of urbanization

Source: Modified from Urban Geoscience (McCall, De Mulder, and Marker, editors)

Construction and functioning of those megacities require huge volumes of building materials and other daily mineral commodities, which all need to be transported. The magnitude of this volume moved by humans equals that of geological processes such as continental drift and erosion.

Massive capital sums are spent to build cities and to maintain their necessary infrastructure. The geological conditions of the underlying soils and rocks control in a large part the cost of building. Other geological events such as sea level rise, changes in river courses, earthquakes, volcanoes, etc. also have a major impact.

A need was created by this shift in human population and the huge capital investments needed to obtain a better understanding. Geology for planning and more specifically, urban geology studies were born to address this demand.

The Economic and Social Commission for Asia and the Pacific (ESCAP) of the United Nations understood early on the demands and specific needs of the Asian region and it started in the 1980s with efforts to promote this new science by publishing the Atlas of Urban Geology series.

Bangkok received attention in the first publications. In the current publication we try to draw some lessons, conclusions and examples of day-to-day impact from the current situation in Bangkok.

The aim is to make the average reader aware that the geologist – often seen as the bearer of bad news – plays a major role in daily city life by helping to reduce and prevent major capital losses.

B. Geology for planning – urban geoscience

Land-use planning on a regional and local scale is a must; market forces alone are unable to cope in a satisfactory way with the need to supply adequate provisions for infrastructure and employment growth.

The purpose of planning is, therefore, to formulate a view about future land-use needs, and then to define optimal solutions. This requires a system of forward planning and the checking of developments against existing plans, prior to issuing permits for particular proposals.

Decisions about the location of development and the extraction of minerals are governed by a variety of planning considerations, which go beyond geological issues, such as economic and social considerations and landscape issues.

Nevertheless, authorities applying good governance must take into account all information available – including geological knowledge – on the date of their decision-making and they should be held accountable for this.

Let us consider an actual case, which took place in Rosella, Hobart, the capital of Tasmania in Australia. A large up-market housing estate was developed in 1990; the project developer obtained all necessary government support and permits. Various banks and finance companies approved the project and provided finance, both to the project developer and the individual house owners. No geological survey was carried out prior to the start of the development of this large and expensive suburb.

Soon after settling in, house owners started to note cracks in their walls, and it was discovered that the soil on which the houses were built moved downhill at a rate of 1mm per four days. Already by 1992, three houses had to be demolished and another thirty were severely damaged. The concerned house owners formed a representative committee, which negotiated with all potentially responsible parties. After employing a geologist it was quickly established – using existing data – and at a cost of merely a few thousand dollars that the whole area had been built on an old landslip. Exploratory drilling with horizontal and vertical holes was carried out to drain the landslip surface at a total cost of about Australian $20,000.

Evidently, the total damages of several million dollars could easily have been avoided by a proper prior survey or by taking appropriate measures at a later stage. Individual home owners were supposed to bear all losses, which caused a lot of personal trauma and financial problems. After many years of active campaigning, using all available means (newspapers, radios, TV, etc.) the Government relented and accepted to bear part of the overall costs together with the various banks and financial institutions, which had been actively involved in the promotion of the housing project.

This demonstration of obvious neglect of good governance by all the parties involved in designing and implementing the project resulted in changes of the law, first across Tasmania and later throughout Australia to enforce the inclusion and study of geological data prior to giving building permits.

1. Geology for planning data

The published geological map is the standard available tool. Using (digitized) maps at various scales, conclusions can be drawn on the possible risks and their mitigation. Common risks include river migration and flooding, landslides, subsidence, caving/karst/collapse of underlying limestone rocks, sea level rise, earth tremors and many others. Appropriate map scales are required to clearly reveal the potential risks.

Remote sensing data, both from aerial surveys and satellite images, further help to understand the local and regional conditions and the possible impact thereof on the development of a building project.

Soil information also is often available from published maps. All of the above-mentioned data can be digitized and integrated using standard Geological Information Systems (GIS). This enables the user to compare different information at the same scale and to overlay it where desired.

Underground data from water bores, geological exploration, mining and geophysical surveys exist but gathering and presenting them in a useable (digitized) format is often problematic.

For a fast-growing city like Bangkok it is a major problem to assemble all subsurface data collected by different authorities and store the data in an accessible digitized format. The problem is even more complex for documents prepared a century ago. For the urban geoscientist the situation is rather frustrating: ample data are available but he lacks the means to access them. Transparency for coordinating information, needed for decision-making remains therefore elusive. Such a situation is certain to lead to unwarranted problems in project development and to additional capital costs.

Geology for planning, though not an active direct science, is used daily to solve problems, which might cause harm to people, property and environment. Presenting the collated data in a format understandable to the concerned parties (local authorities, engineers, architects, project developers, etc., who can then use them in their decision-making) is among the main tasks for this discipline.

A typical case is the construction of a dam site. A geological map also showing various soil types and cultivation practices provides an immediate overview of the potential gains and losses from such a venture. Various projects have been constructed in Thailand, which would not have been carried out if sufficient data had been available and presented in an accessible format to the decision-making authorities.

The cost of data collection, manipulation and presentation is negligeable, compared to the total budget allocated, but of truly fundamental value.

With the growing use of interlinked databases, it is likely that interpreted maps can be made available to the public at cost via the Internet, so that each concerned person may check these data and draw his or her own conclusions. Setting up such a service requires a well-coordinated effort by the various government authorities. Once established it may well be worth privatizing the service to cover its startup and running costs (see also chapter J).

2. Urban geology and ESCAP

In the 1960s and 1970s it became common knowledge amongst large geological companies that multidisciplinary teams offer greater cost-benefits and better results. ESCAP noted this new approach in the commercial geological community early on and decided to adopt this principal into its own work programme to increase the value of its monetary resources invested for the benefit of the community it serves.

The main scientific sectors combined in this multidisciplinary team approach were Geology, Geography, Water Resources Management, Natural Disaster Mitigation, Planning, Civil Engineering and Information Technology, amongst others. The aim was to provide a way of thinking beneficial to all people living in the ESCAP region.

After having been provided with some examples, several member countries started their own work. It soon became clear that scientists could work together using this multidisciplinary approach. The results being very encouraging, provided an important message to all planners and government authorities responsible for planning.

Scientists of various disciplines have been convinced of the benefit of working together in the field of urban geology. Published results have been well received and created nuclei of motivated scientists and government officials in various countries from which national initiatives did grow.

Presently we aim to show a larger public what these results may mean to them. Translating this scientific approach into common knowledge is important if we are to succeed in deriving the maximum benefit for all.

The Atlas of Urban Geology series was an ESCAP initiative started in 1988. Twelve atlases have since been published and some are under preparation. Prior to this, some selected papers on

Geology for Urban Planning in the Asian and Pacific Region were issued. Those publications aim to show the general public what has been achieved, what are the cost-benefit ratios and how this work touches all of us (see also chapter H).

Urbanization is an ages old process, which grew very fast with the introduction of modern industries. In the developed world this process was relatively slow, though major problems and costly mistakes still occurred, witness the above-mentioned example from Tasmania, Australia. But in Asia, where nearly two thirds of the world population lives, urbanization started later and grew extremely fast. In most countries this very fast urbanization growth continues.

Geology for Planning aims to guide this growth and to alleviate the problems, which may occur. Our environment is a direct function of the geological conditions and the way we use it. Without taking into account basic geology, major, costly, mistakes will be made in city development. In the end we all pay for these errors, so please lets try to avoid them.

Discussions are made on all scales, development of airports, main road system, harbors, river flood controls, ground water use, waste management, sewerage systems, building of houses (including your own), for all of those we must know what are we doing and what are the risks for ourselves and others. Urban Geology offers this opportunity at a relative low cost to all of us.

C. Urban expansion, geological management

The strongest growth in urbanization takes place in developing countries, especially in Africa and South and South-East Asia. ESCAP (1990a) showed that urban population growth varied from 2.16% in China, through 4.18% in Indonesia to 6.18% in Nepal. It is estimated that fifty per cent of the current world population of 7 billion people lives in cities. Sixty cities already have more than 5 million inhabitants each.

Hence 3.5 billion people live in cities, occupying less than one per cent of the Earth's land surface. Seibold (1989) estimated the amount of earth materials removed at about 20 tons per head. This volume is comparable to geological processes such as sedimentation, erosion and continental plate movements. Humans have become a major geological agent.

Urbanization takes place on land, where geological conditions affect and control its destiny. In each city, major investments are made in construction and infrastructure development. Piling and foundation costs form a large part of the overall investment, directly linked to sub-soil geological conditions. Usage of natural building stone – steadily increasing to about 10-15% of hard building materials – is another major geology-related urban investment. Infrastructure development, water distribution systems, sewerage, ground and surface water management, road building, port and airport developments are all controlled by geological environmental conditions.

Multidisciplinary teams combining in-depth knowledge of all technical engineering aspects, planning and geology are the only proper way to manage these huge investments in the urbanization process. The appropriate way to present the processed data on urbanized areas are thematic maps that provide the key to proper management. Urban geologists have to clearly show the economic impact that can be expected by any planned development in a certain area.

D. Urban geology and you

People generally fail to grasp the daily effects and costs, which are related to urban decision-making. One looks at disasters elsewhere, but potential problems at home are often ignored. This attitude – ignoring known facts and unwilling to invest funds for proper investigations – does result in high costs to society but also to the individual. Who is to blame in the end, and who is paying for the problem at that stage? The answer: you are the one presented the bill in the end.

Common practical problems are: landslides, ground subsidence, sewerage pollution, erosion, water shortages, stormwater management, piling, road maintenance, earthquakes and many others. Most geotechnical expenditure goes to foundations, mainly for low-rise buildings. Commonly up to ten per cent of actual costs is spent on remedial work.

The main elements affecting living in an urban setting are summarized below:

- Transport of solid materials to the city
- Soil conditions
- Groundwater
- Natural and man-made hazards
- Availability and use of building materials
- Urban development conditions & constraints

These topics will be discussed under the following headings, where applicable samples and actual situations will be addressed.

1. Transport of solid materials to the city

A large agglomeration like Bangkok needs a daily influx of materials to function. A United Nations study showed a consumption of nearly 20 tons/annum per head (see table I.1).

Table I.1. Estimated annual consumption of mineral commodities by a city of 250,000 people

(based on figures presented at various times by G.W. Lüttig & F.C. Wolff)

Mineral commodity	Tons per annum
Sand and gravel	1 650 000
Hard Rock	500 000
Petroleum	600 000
Coal	500 000
Limestone	350 000
Steel	50 000
Cement	25 000
Clays	100 000
Industrial sands	80 000
Rock salt	50 000
Gypsum	20 000
Dolomite	2 500
Phosphate	2 000
Sulphur	7 000
Peat	6 500
Natural freestone	6 500
Potash salts	6 000
Aluminium	5 000
Kaolin	4 000
Copper	3 500

Source: Urban Geoscience (McCall, De Mulder, and Marker editors)

Figure I.2. Heavy trucks transporting rocks or sand to the city cause dust, pollution and road damage

Standard aggregates such as sand, gravel, hard rock, and limestone form the bulk of the materials transported. Taking the official number of about 6 million people populating Bangkok this would mean roughly 60 million tons per year or 8,000 truckloads of 20 tons per day. Transport of this huge volume takes place by riverboat, train and trucks. One can just imagine the effect of hundreds of trucks on each road leading to the city, day after day. Intensive infrastructure planning to handle these massive transport requirements is a decisive factor determining the success of such a metropolis.

The effects of mining of such vast quantities are considerable. The adverse effects of mineral exploration are numerous and complex. The limestone mountains located 100-150 km outside Bangkok do supply the majority of the required hard materials. The effect is enormous (see pictures), whole mountains have disappeared. One of the major consequences of the mining, besides the destruction of the environment, is the huge amount of dust released into the atmosphere. Rehabilitation of the ravaged landscape at a later stage is needed so future development can take place on this abandoned land.

Planning of major haulage ways is critical in optimizing the social, environmental and maintenance costs. Knowledge of soil and subsoil conditions is the key factor for such infrastructure development planning. Building of roads on a soft underground is only feasible at high costs, the alternative is to repeatedly repair the cracks caused by subsidence and vibration settlement difference in the subsoil (see figures I.5, I.13 and I.14). Either way requires high capital outlays, which should be set against the low cost of carrying out an adequate geological survey, providing hard data for a balanced decision making process.

Figure I.3. Large-scale extraction of construction materials to build the city
leads to local environmental degradation without proper controls

2. Urbanization and soils

Urbanization takes place mainly in prosperous agricultural areas with good links to other areas or around major mining developments. An irreversible loss of soil as an agricultural resource results from the urbanization process. Soils are buried beneath buildings, roads and other forms of infrastructure and are often severely contaminated by industrial or other waste. Enclosed undisturbed areas are often exposed to a range of environmental pressures, which destroy their effective function.

The European Environment Agency (1995) estimates that two per cent of Europe's agricultural land is lost to urbanization every ten years. Rapid urbanization in Asia and the forming of huge agglomerations as, e.g., in coastal areas of eastern China takes place mainly in coastal lowlands previously used for agriculture.

In most cases know-how of the soil conditions is limited to rural soils. Soil mapping and research is mainly limited to guide agricultural and forest development. Knowledge of urban soils is often limited. Social studies have demonstrated the need for a minimum amount of open green space in cities. These green spaces also improve the urban climate by increased air circulation, noise and dust reduction, humidity control, and rainwater absorption. Known soil conditions will guide the decision makers to select areas for parks, which are not well suited for other developments.

An urban park of 1 hectare can remove up to 900 kg of CO_2 from the air and deliver 600 kg of oxygen within a 12-hour period. Planning of adequate green space in city space near polluted areas (high traffic density) is a clear must. Statistics compiled by the European Commission on open space and green areas shows large differences (see table I.2).

Fast-growing cities like Bangkok, spreading fast into the surrounding agricultural area have vast areas of unused open space in its suburbs. Even in the developed areas large areas remain in private gardens belonging to older dwelling and undeveloped plots. The area set aside for public parks is limited.

Table I.2. Proportion of total city area occupied by open space and proportion of the open area regarded as green space *(data adapted from European Commission, 1995)*

City	Open space per cent	Open space as green space per cent	Green space within city area per cent
Amsterdam	7	23	1
Barcelona	40	58	23
Brussels	35	66	23
Glasgow	29	13	4
Hannover	50	50	25
London	n/a	10	–
Milan	58	18	10
Paris	23	92	21
Vienna	68	50	34
Zurich	67	80	54

Source: Urban Geoscience (McCall, De Mulder, and Marker editors)

3. Urban soil management

Soil performs a number of important functions such as: elemental recycling; medium for plant growth; water drainage and distribution; habitat for soil fauna and flora; as well as being a resource for construction purposes. Urbanization affects the soil in many ways. Good management may preserve natural soil. Loss of soil will be caused by burial, erosion and environmental damage. During construction much soil is moved, with some high quality topsoil being sold for soil improvement. However, most soil ends up in landfills.

In low-lying areas such as in Bangkok, landfill is necessary to bring the surface above flood level. The original soil is thus buried underneath. The entire area is then compacted, reducing the soil bulk density, which in turn restricts root development and water circulation. Water penetration and circulation will become restricted when the area is covered with concrete or bitumen, making it difficult for trees to grow. Soils, which do not have a vegetation cover, and particularly those with low organic matter content, are prone to surface damage caused by the impact of raindrops. The dispersion of small soil particles will clog the pore space in the upper part (mm-cm) of the soil profile. This surface capping further restricts the penetration of water.

Both soil profiles mentioned above result in high run-off and subsequent erosion. Overall urban activities lead to compaction, even in park lands this often happens. Passage of heavy equipment over loose soil – especially when wet – causes compaction. Compaction often leads to poor drainage, which excludes earthworms and other soil organisms from the area, further resulting in high run-off and erosion.

The lack of aeration and drainage in these compacted soils blocks the growing of roots and causes trees to die. Reclamation of such compacted soils is often very difficult and requires digging up and replacing the soil.

The mapping of urban soils, followed by making this information available on thematic maps will help all concerned take into account the various soil types and identify those most suitable for particular uses. Preventing unnecessary soil burial and compaction during construction activities – by careful stripping and storage of material at this stage – will alleviate many problems.

Proper data collection and careful soil management will greatly reduce both the cost of maintenance and the environmental impact of urban soils. Especially in areas with monsoon rain, poor quality soils blocking water penetration result in water logging, high run-offs, flooding and erosion.

4. Urban water management

Urban growth relies on adequate water supply. This supply for private consumption and industrial usage must be assured to guarantee sustainable urban development.

Initially water is derived from surface resources and limited groundwater supplies, but soon consumption of groundwater increases, often to become the main reliable source. As such a development is unsustainable, water is collected in reservoirs and piped to the agglomeration. This results in lowering the city's dependence on groundwater supplies. However, private consumers tend to increase their groundwater consumption, either because no piped water from the mains is available or because it is perceived to be much cheaper (see box).

Several main aspects play an important role in this development scenario:

1. Groundwater characteristics,
    a) Pumping – subsidence
    b) Sanitation – pollution
    c) Coning – clogging
2. Water distribution/consumption
    a) Leakage
    b) Discharge
    c) Effects
3. Sewerage effects
    a) Leakage
    b) Discharge/private
4. Subsidence
    a) Housing/construction
    b) Compaction
    c) Infiltration of salt water
5. Recharging of groundwater
    a) Change in consumption
    b) Effects

The following subsections will discuss these topics and relate them to relevant examples in Bangkok or other cities.

---

5 Billion baht [US $110 million] sought to stem land subsidence

But science ministry opposes the project

The Industry Ministry plans to request nearly five billion baht from the Environment Fund to "recharge" aquifer storage to stem land subsidence after failing to control groundwater consumption by industry in crisis areas. Deputy Industry Minister Preecha Laohapongchana wants to use the money to build 50 stations in Bangkok and surrounding provinces to inject water underground in an attempt to prop up the land. Each station will cost about 95 million baht while the operational cost is about a million baht a day. The Department of Mineral Resources (DMR) says clean surplus water during the rainy season will be pumped into groundwater layers. But the Office of Environmental Policy and Planning at the Science, Technology and Environment Ministry, which administers the fund, has been reluctant to go along with the project. "A feasibility study must be undertaken before a decision is made due to the high investment cost. We have found that the subsidence rate has declined," said science permanent secretary Santhad Somchivita.

Overuse of groundwater is the main cause of land subsidence, and industry is the main user. A survey last year found that there were 33,995 factories in Bangkok and surrounding provinces. Together they have used 1.5 million cubic metres (m^3) out of 2.5 million m^3 of water pumped from underground aquifers each year in recent years. Officials said the capacity of Bangkok aquifers to supply groundwater was about a million m^3 a day. But water pumped up should be less than capacity to prevent land subsidence. Overconsumption of groundwater led to the promulgation of the Ground Water Act in 1978 to try to impose some control but it was in vain.

During 1978-88, land in Bangkok sank more than 70 centimetres. The worst affected area was Ramkhamhaeng which sank 85.3 cm and now is 4 cm below mean sea level. Because of the seriousness of the situation, the cabinet issued a resolution in March 1983 to impose stringent controls on designated "crisis areas". In the same year, the DMR began charging the consumption of groundwater from industries in an attempt to discourage its use. But the measure failed because the price charged for ground water was much less than that for alternative sources of water. For example, the Provincial Waterworks Authority recently privatized a water plant in Pathum Thani to serve residents and industrial plants: However, factories continued to pump up water from artesian wells because it cost only 3.5 baht for each m^3 compared to 21 baht charged by the water company. This situation has led the PWA to urge the DMR to prohibit factories in its service areas from using groundwater. But the initiative has run into stiff opposition from the federation of Thai industries.

– *Bangkok Post by Kanittha Inchukul (24 Jan. 1999)*

(i)   Groundwater characteristics

　　a.   Groundwater consumption and its effects

Rapid growth of a city like Bangkok in a monsoon climate requires the utilization of its groundwater resources to satisfy consumption. Initially the water authority placed the main bores and monitored the effects. Once it became clear that demand outstripped supply other solution were implemented. However industrial and private consumption increased their reliance on their own bores. The water drawn from them is often much cheaper than the one piped in. Also in areas where none or insufficient piped water is available, private bores proliferate.

The effect is a rapid decline of the groundwater level up to 80 m in Bangkok, where it is estimated that over 900 million cubic metres of groundwater are extracted each year.

The drawing of groundwater affects its flow regime. Increased flow rates may cause pore space clogging rendering the system impermeable. Groundwater can either be recharged quickly in a permeable or porous geological system, e.g., alluvial deposits, or very slowly in consolidated bedrock. Recharge may take place either as a natural process or by injecting water through boreholes.

Lowering of the groundwater table leads to – often permanent – soil compaction, especially of the clay layers. Compaction in its turn causes subsidence. Subsidence may vary according to the underlying configuration of the sub-soil layers.

Sewerage systems are often lacking in the early city development stages. Sanitation system can have a significant impact on shallow aquifers that underlie a city, as a result of leakage and/or seepage. This may lead to a deterioration of the water resource.

The coning effect, caused by pumping over a long period, changes water flows. Both chemical and physical parameters of the soil may be altered. Fine particles may block pore space and lower the permeability. Chemical elements (pollutants) may be carried by the flows and concentrate in certain levels.

A major risk is the infiltration of (salt) seawater in coastal areas. In case the salt water fills up the vacated space it may destroy much of the soil for agricultural use, leaving only a thin veneer of fresh surface water on the top, separating the top layer from the deeper fresh water aquifers.

Figure I.4. Discharge of a modern sewerage plant

b. Water distribution

Most major cities have a water distribution system, which serves most housing and industrial complexes. Often sub-standard housing districts (slums) and squatter areas are poorly served. Published data, (see table I.3), show percentages of less than 50 per cent of the population being connected to the mains.

Table I.3. Urban population with access to water supply and sanitation
(source: Lea and Courtney, 1986)

indicator	City			
	Metro Manila	*Jakarta*	*Calcutta*	*Madras*
Total population (millions)	6.4	8	9.2	5
Area (km²)	646	550	800	1 170
Urban density (cap/ha)	98	200	115	43
Population in sub-standard housing (slums)	45	40	33	60
% Living in squatter-illegal settlements	30	n/a	n/a	25
% With access to water (house connections)	43	47	48	40
% Garbage collected daily	70	25	55	78
% Human access to human waste disposal system	60	42	45	58

Source: Urban Geoscience (McCall, De Mulder and Marker, editors)

In Bangkok the water distributed yearly (1999) from the Chao Phraya Basin was about 1,415 million cubic metres (Bangkok Post). This huge amount corresponds to the volume of several major storage dams, leaving less water for agricultural purposes.

Water distribution systems are often old and buried rather deep. As all pipes are pressurized, leaking forms a major problem. Studies reveal an average loss of 20-30 per cent in European cities, in Bangkok it reaches 40 per cent and in Hanoi even 50 per cent.

Taking the Bangkok figures, about 560 million cubic metres are lost each year due to leaking pipes. Assuming a surface of about 600 square kilometres for the served area, this corresponds to 1,000 mm rainfall. The recharge of the groundwater from leaking pipes is greater than from annual rainfall, which also runs off to a large extent.

Old pipes were laid in Bangkok over 150 years ago and were made of thick steel and laid in deep soils. Most leakage is through pipe connections, which are normally located at every five to six metres. The problem is exacerbated by soft soil and numerous construction projects causing differential settlement. Traffic, soil compaction and subsidence aggravate the differential compaction and movement of the soil and pipes. Currently in Bangkok mainly PVC pipes are used instead of stainless steel ones, as is the custom in e.g. Singapore and Japan. Obviously, leaking is not restricted to Bangkok city but also occurs in the surrounding provinces.

c. Sewerage and sanitation effects

Sewerage systems, where available, collect wastewater and bring it to treatment areas. Sullage ponds may leak if not properly sealed. The cleaned water is normally collected in ponds from which recharging of the groundwater takes place, while overflow is disposed off via natural waterways.

As sewerage pipes are not pressurized, leakage is usually limited. Nevertheless, old pipes in the inner city area are often damaged, allowing infiltration of the sewerage into the groundwater system.

Figure I.5. Cracking of the road surface around installed drainage inlets

Many dwellings and industrial compounds are not connected to the sewerage collection system. A mixture of several waste disposal systems is used, e.g., septic tanks, settlement ponds, etc. These systems may work well, but failures are common, causing leakage. Overflows are often directly discharged into the rivers or the sea.

Studies show that in general only 5-10 per cent of distributed water is used for consumption. The remainder is used for waste/industrial purposes. Taking into account only the distributed water in Bangkok, about 770 million cubic metres are potential groundwater recharge. If a significant proportion of the water supply is obtained from local groundwater, large-scale recycling will occur, whereas if a significant proportion is obtained from external sources, there will be a substantial increase in net groundwater recharge. Obviously the sedimentological spatial distribution controls the flow of this injected pumped water, ending up as groundwater recharge or in the surface water system.

In case of shallow water tables during the rainy season, disposal of domestic wastewater to the ground via on-site systems is not always possible. Under these conditions septic tanks overflow directly into surface watercourses via open drains. Obviously, recharge is much reduced under such conditions, although groundwater recharge from the open canals still takes place.

Overall it is clear that un-sewered sanitation greatly increases the rate of urban groundwater recharge.

Industrial activities often located in the suburban areas generate liquid effluents, such as spent lubricants, solvents and disinfectants, which are often discharged directly into the soil posing a serious threat to groundwater quality. Larger industrial sites have their own ponds for handling and storing of wastewaters. Often these shallow oxidation lagoons are unlined with high rates of loss through seepage with a potentially big impact on the local groundwater recharge.

(ii)   Subsidence

As mentioned above, continuous pumping leads to a lower water table (-80 m in Bangkok). This lowering of the water table causes a soil dewatering with subsequent compaction. Especially in an alluvial deltaic setting with marine clay interbeds, such as in Bangkok, many clay horizons are interspersed between sandy bars. Clays may loose up to 90 per cent of their volume if they dry out completely prior to consolidating into solid rock. By lowering the water table several tens of meters, compaction may also be measured finally in tens of meters. For a near-coastal city like Bangkok this poses a major risk. Known subsidence over the last 60 years is estimated at nearly two metres, and current annual rates vary from 1.5 to 5.3 cm (see figure I.10).

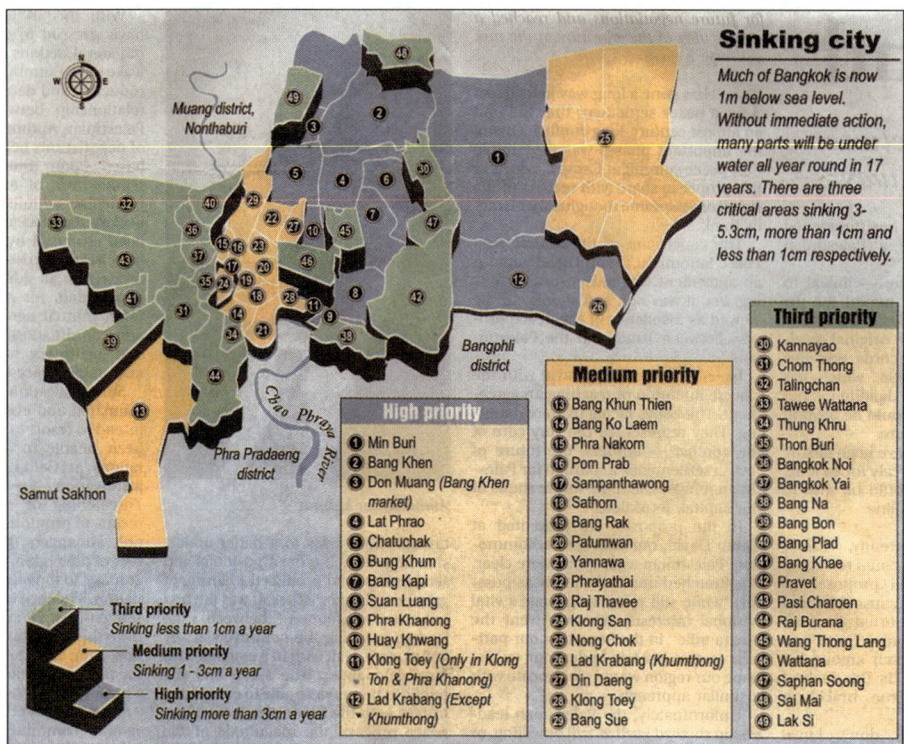

Figure I.6. **Bangkok, the sinking city** *(source: Bangkok Post, August 6, 2000)*

Only detailed research on the clay horizons can reveal if compaction is reversible. Certain clays (swelling type) can absorb the water again if they become submerged. However if the mineralogy has been changed shrinking becomes irreversible. Detailed study of the thickness of the clay beds, their composition and water content is required to answer these questions.

It is a normal geological event that sediments in floodplains compact due to increased loading. This is balanced by flooding and new sediment distribution by the river. Subsidence caused by lowering the water table is a human-induced hazard, further enhanced by artificially controlling the river flow, so that flooding with an associated new sediment built-up is no longer taking place.

E. Bangkok urban geological data

1. Bangkok coastal location – a historical perspective

Geological history shows ongoing transgression (i.e., sea covering land) and regression (land drying up) events. These shore movements can be caused by structural movements (uplift of the entire region) or by relative sea level changes. It is extremely difficult to determine which factors are the main ones in the Earth's history.

Figure I.7. Subsidence: original surface was at the bottom of the door

Well known ice ages have caused big changes in relative sea levels. Climatic changes control the rainfall and subsequent river flows, erosion and sediment deposition.

The Gulf of Thailand was dry during the last ice age (~20,000 years ago). Melting of the ice and rising sea levels caused a rapid transgression which saw the shoreline moving up to at least 100 kilometres north of Bangkok (~7,000 years ago). Since the Tertiary, the entire region subsided rapidly, and mainly fluviatile sediments filled it in. These sediments are host to the major oil and gas fields in the Thai offshore basins, demonstrating clearly that transgression and regression took place since that time.

Seashore changes depend on the geological subsidence, sea level changes and sedimentation rates. Hotly debated global warming-cum-sea level changes may change climatic conditions. The dramatic climatic differences between El Niño and La Niña are known to all of us.

Figure I.8. Dike to protect mangrove forest, Bangkok shoreline

Storm activity is also a direct result of climate conditions. Shoreline profiles over the last few hundred years reveal that it prograded rapidly until mid last century and remained stable thereafter. This suggests that the delta today is in equilibrium.

The sea level rise as postulated will translate into a rapid transgression. The artificially lowered water table with its deep cone underneath Bangkok will allow seawater to fill this vacant space. Moreover, if subsidence continues unabated and no protective structures are built, most or the entire area will be inundated. Thus, a normal geological process will be severely enhanced by human-induced changes.

**Figure I.9. Looking across eroded shoreline, with local transgression of 5 m/annum.
Protected land in the background**

Mangrove forests protect most of the shoreline in the Gulf of Thailand. The uncontrolled destruction of these forests has changed the equilibrium between deposition and erosion caused by alongshore currents. The mangrove forests no longer block erosive wave action during the dry season, resulting in rapid landward erosion (exceeding 5 m per year).

2. Bangkok geology

The Bangkok metropolis is located in the northern tip of the Gulf of Thailand, which formed as a pull-apart basin, following the northwesterly trending regional wrench faulting.

The Three Pagodas Fault system, passing under Bangkok is one of these northwesterly wrench fault zones. As a result of the regional movements, North-South trending normal block faulting occurs. The Chao Phraya River follows such a fault with a down-warp of over 1,000 m at its western side. Today's anticipated changes to the local environment are minimal to what transpired in the recent past.

Sediment shedding takes place all along the mountains forming the border between Thailand and Myanmar. Uplift of this mountain range is a result of tectonic plate movement. Basin faults are also reactivated by these crustal displacements, leading to an ongoing subsidence.

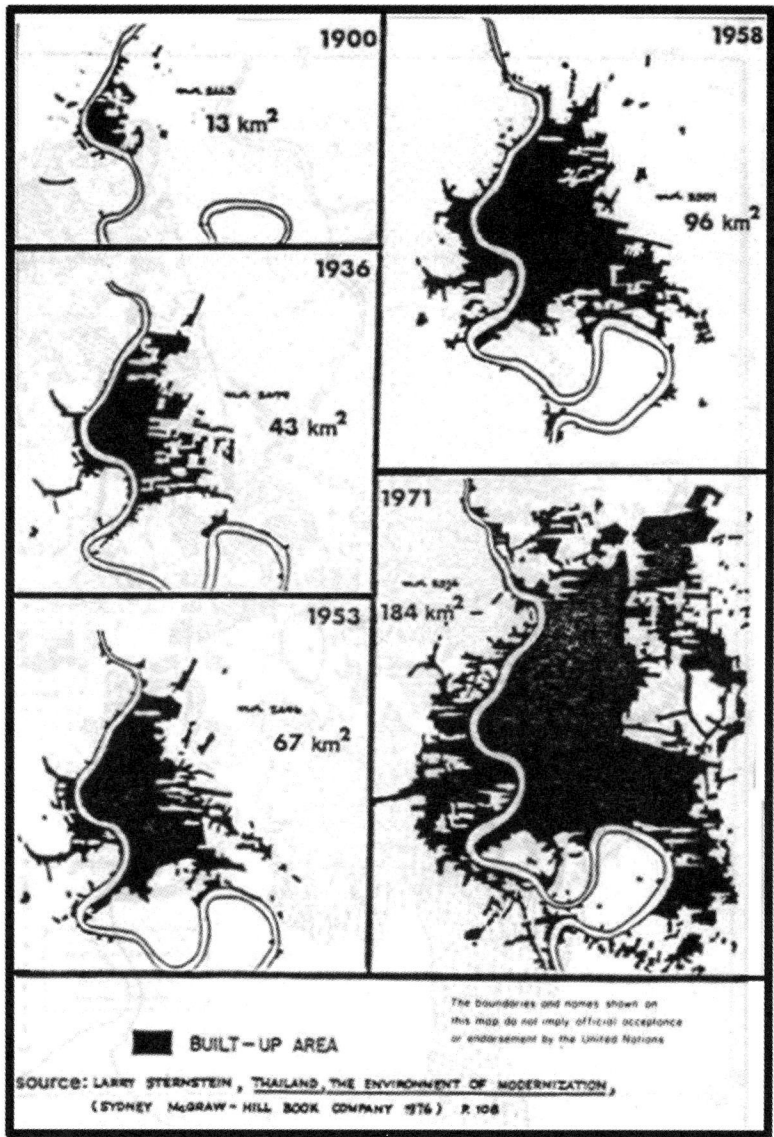

Figure I.10. Growth of Bangkok *(Atlas of Urban Geology 5)*

Infill of the Gulf of Thailand shows a paralic sedimentary sequence comprising fluviatile, deltaic, tidal and marine units.

The soft sediments under Bangkok are known from the numerous water wells drilled. A simplified stratigraphic table is shown as figure I.12.

It is obvious that each aquifer represents a fluviatile deltaic sequence with interfingering silt/clay beds representing tidal flat deposits. Each complete sedimentary sequence is fining upwards and covered by marine clays. Successive erosion may have removed this top section. Basin-wide lateral variations probably cause contacts between the various sand layers. It is important to realize that coarse sediments are laid down in a relative short time interval, as limited winnowing has been described, but large laterally known clay deposits represent much larger intervals.

The top zone of figure I.12 shows 5 distinct sedimentary cycles. It can safely be postulated that these cycles, each about 50-60 m thick, are the result of structural activity (uplift), which caused shedding of coarse sediments.

Currently we are at the end or the start of a new cycle. Marine Holocene clay has been deposited and now rivers are eroding into this layer. The river incises into flood plains when the sea level drops. Once the incision reaches a level that is subject to flooding, the flood plain becomes inactive. Data shows that the river used to follow a more easterly coarse before migrating to its current location.

Superimposed on the observed repetition of sedimentary cycles we have worldwide trans- and regressions related to sea level changes. Transgression causes the drowning of the fluviatile system, by covering it up with clays. Glacial cycles have caused several trans- and regressions since the Pleistocene.

Figure I.11. Reshaped oxbow lake, an old meander of the Chao Phraya River

The Bangkok surface layer of about 20 m consists of marine clays covering tidal flats. Little is known about the spatial distributions in this clay layer. Visual observations show intercalated organic lenses, and silty to fine sand channels. Lack of detailed information makes it impossible to draw proper thematic maps providing necessary data for infrastructure development.

Each fluviatile cycle hosts its individual connate ground water. Spatial distribution suggests that lateral communication between the different units is likely. Fractures, bore holes and irregular subsidence may further enhance the exchange between the different water systems. Increased pressure differences caused by pumping in certain areas will stimulate inter-unit flows. Contained local chemical pollution may thus be spread over large areas.

3. Pumping impact

The Bangkok topsoil surface consists of marine clay (Bangkok clay) with a thickness of 10-30 m. This clay is soft and easily compressible. Interstitial salt water is released slowly during compaction. The clay may shrink up to 10 per cent of its original volume before becoming solid claystone.

Based on information from bore logs a total of 8 principal artesian aquifers are distinguished in the upper most 600 m. Thick clay or sandy clay horizons related to marine transgressions separate these units (figure I.12).

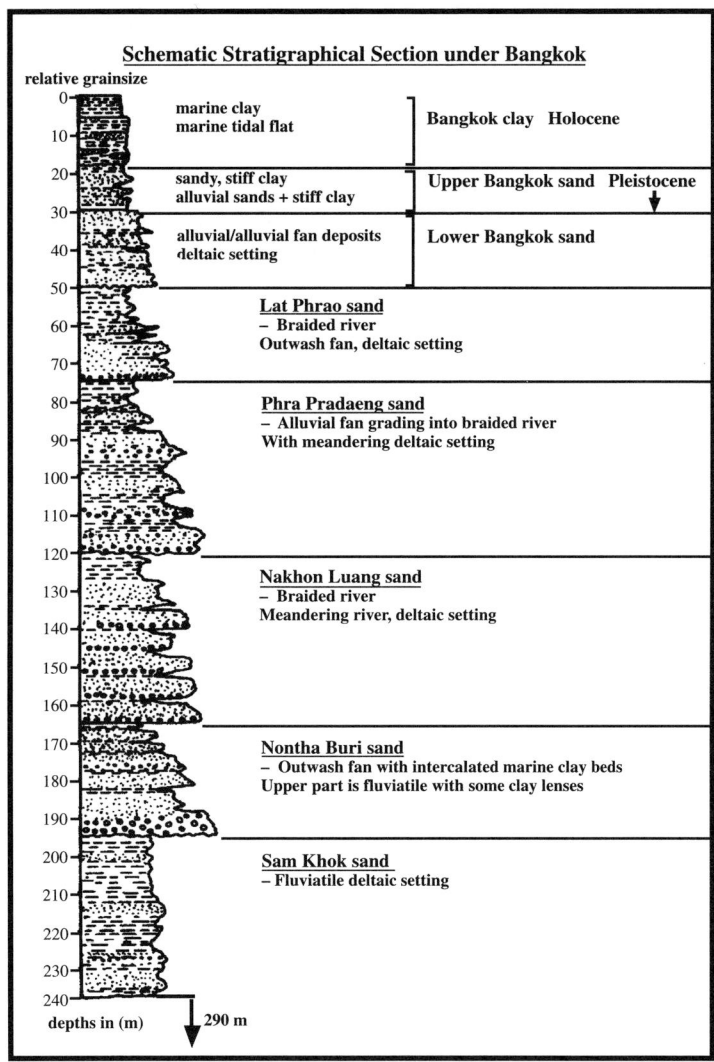

Figure I.12. Schematic stratigraphic section underlying Bangkok

Water from the first sandy layer of Bangkok sand is undrinkable due to high salinity. The 2nd (Phra Pradaeng 100 m zone), 3rd (Nakhon Luang 150 m) and 4th (Nontha Buri 200 m) are the main aquifers for Bangkok. The deeper ones Sam Khok (300 m) and Phaya Thai (350 m) are increasingly used in the Pathum Thani province (North-West of Bangkok). The 7th (Thon Buri 450 m) and 8th (Pak Nam 550 m) aquifers are used only for industrial purposes in the areas South and South-West of Bangkok, where there is no alternative overlying aquifer.

As mentioned above, the sedimentological configuration is a direct result from regional geological depositional changes in the Gulf of Thailand region.

4. Groundwater management discussion

The Bangkok situation is retained for discussion. The main elements are summarized as follows:

Estimated annual groundwater pumped	900 million m^3
Piped annual water	1,415 million m^3
Annual water leakage	560 million m^3
Sewerage/sanitation annual waste	770 million m^3
Annual rainfall 600-km^2/1,000 mm	600 million m^3

The picture is quite complex. Groundwater use is larger than the recharge-taking place. This has caused a deep cone over the central Bangkok where the water table has been lowered considerably.

Hydrological regional flows from inland to the sea recharge the groundwater. These flows are rather slow. Further direct recharge may result from the water pipe leakage. Leaking and pumping are not necessarily at the same locations. Sewerage/sanitation waste is also very large and a considerable quantity may enter into the groundwater resource. Potentially this recharge may introduce an environmental pollution risk. Detailed study is required to determine how much of this introduced water reaches the used aquifers. It may well be that most of it enters the upper Bangkok sand layer, which is not used as a groundwater resource.

Increased gradient water flows, transporting fine particles, towards the cone will infill pore space and will lead to a permanent decrease in permeability and porosity. Also, soluble pollutants will be distributed over a larger area by these increased flow rates. Depending on the physical chemical conditions (pH and Eh) precipitation of these chemical compounds may take place in various horizons.

Fresh water has a lower density than salt water. Once the cone caused by over extraction reaches a lower (captive) salt water level, this will rise rapidly to fill the empty space. Similar the seawater may penetrate inland once the fresh water table becomes lower than the seawater table and permeable passageways are created.

Much of the urban recharge derives from natural recharge from rainfall and surface waters besides the leakage of water pipes and disposed sanitation/sewerage water. A considerable amount of pollutants are introduced into the groundwater by the sanitation/sewerage discharge.

The unconsolidated soil on which Bangkok is built consists mainly of clay, salt and sands. By removing the free groundwater, the sediments will compact and this higher density causes interstitial pore water to be released. As a result of this, certain clays may be reduced to 10 per cent of their original volume. This is a normal geological process and overall equilibrium is normally maintained by sediment loading on the top by the active river systems. Human influence increases the compaction process and blocks river movements and its sediment deposition. This results in an increased subsidence not compensated by new surface deposits. Rate of current subsidence varies between 2 and 6 metres per century.

Figure I.13. Cracks appear at the foot of buildings due to subsidence and compaction of the top layers

Figure I.14. Cracks appearing at bridge/road linkages, as bridges stand on piles while roads are built on shrinking subsoil

Historically the seashore in the Bangkok region has moved considerable distances North and South due to geological influences. The currently forecasted sea level rise due to global warming is estimated at between about 50 cm and 3 m over the next century. Destruction of the mangrove forest protection along the coastline enhances the erosion; the coastline currently is moving inland at 5 m per year (see figures I.8 and I.9).

Knowing all these facts, it is certainly feasible to protect the urbanized area by building an adequate dyke system. However, a major problem will be to prevent salt water penetrating and replacing the diminishing fresh groundwater. Obviously the key is in stopping excessive pumping, as the recharge from natural flows, leaking pipes and the sewerage/sanitation wastewaters (if sufficient communication exists) will enable the groundwater table to rise quickly.

In addition it is technically feasible to inject water to replenish the deleted groundwater, or to built reservoirs from which groundwater may be recharged. Considering the nature of the Bangkok soil with many clay beds, penetration rates from the surface are often low. Much of the water collected during the rainy season will run-off naturally.

Both schemes are very expensive, as the biggest problems occur in the built-up areas where land is expensive and access to water limited.

Replenishing the depleted groundwater will cause the water table to rise again. It is known from various older industrial European cities that after excessive pumping stopped (mainly due to the

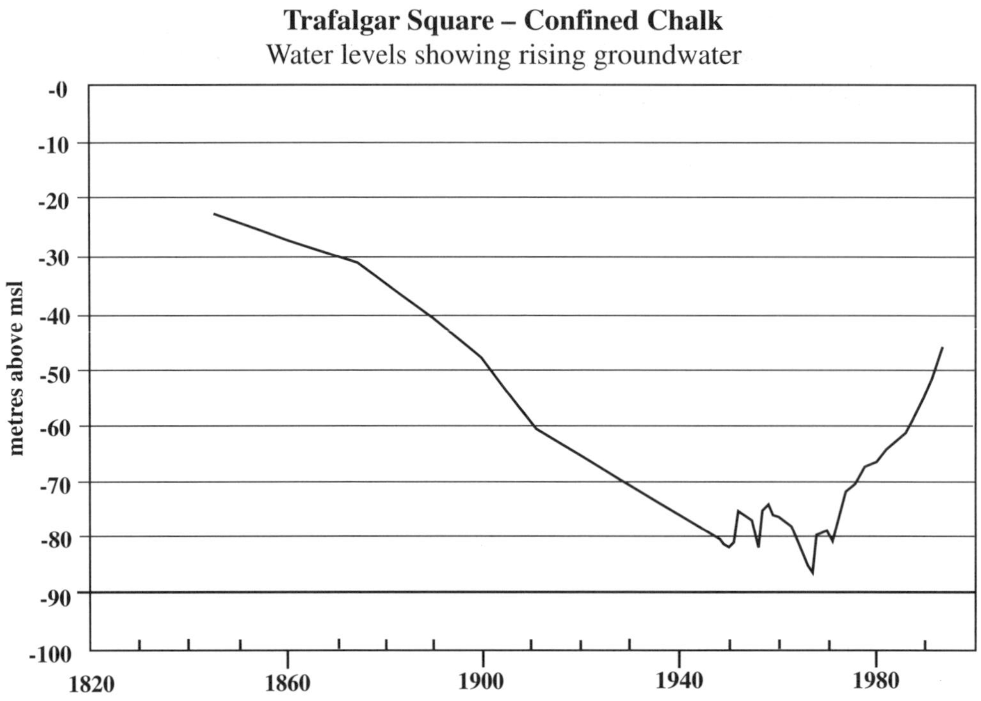

Trafalgar Square – Confined Chalk
Water levels showing rising groundwater

Figure I.15. Groundwater level rise in the Chalk aquifer beneath London (1970-1995)

Source: Urban Geoscience (McCall, De Mulder, and Marker editors)

declining inner city industrial activity) the groundwater level started to rise. Recharge came also from leakages and sewerage/sanitation sources besides the natural one (see figure I.15).

Rising groundwater poses yet another risk. Clay beds may be susceptible to swelling causing soil movement. This disruptive soil movement may affect underground pipes, tunnels, and piling. Contaminated soils may release their toxic component, which is redeposited in the higher levels near the surface.

Figure 1.16. Building up roads to compensate for subsidence causes elevation problems at crossings

**Figure I.17. Rebuilt road, about 50 cm higher than adjacent land,
causing flooding problems during the rainy season**

All of the above demonstrates – in a nutshell – the magnitude of the problems faced in the management of groundwater. A multidisciplinary approach is the only way to classify all elements and to identify the most practical solutions. Just keep in mind the effect on high-rise buildings if their pilings are affected by swelling clays, causing lateral displacements.

F. Hazards

1. Introduction

Urbanization leads to a very high concentration of people in a small area. Disasters, such as earthquakes, volcanic eruptions, tsunamis or tidal waves, storms, and river flooding, are the main hazards related to geological conditions.

Human-related disasters, such as plane crashes, fires and chemical pollution, also represent a real risk. The mitigation of the latter is a direct result of a proper enforcement of government regulations, but a certain risk always remains. Natural disasters are much more difficult to mitigate. Proper understanding of the risk involves the development of measures to be ready for such an event. Implementing these safety measures is expensive; requirements need to be balanced against the economic cost and the perceived risk.

2. Bangkok assessment

The main natural hazards are earthquakes or tremors, floods and storms. Human-induced hazards are not discussed in this context.

(i)   Earthquakes

To assess the risk we need to evaluate the regional structural setting of Bangkok. In the Early Miocene (20 million years ago – see figure I.18) the resulting effect of the stress along the left lateral moving Red River Fault (North Viet Nam) and the right lateral moving Three Pagodas Fault (Central Thailand) systems led to the opening of the Gulf of Thailand. By the Middle Miocene (15 million

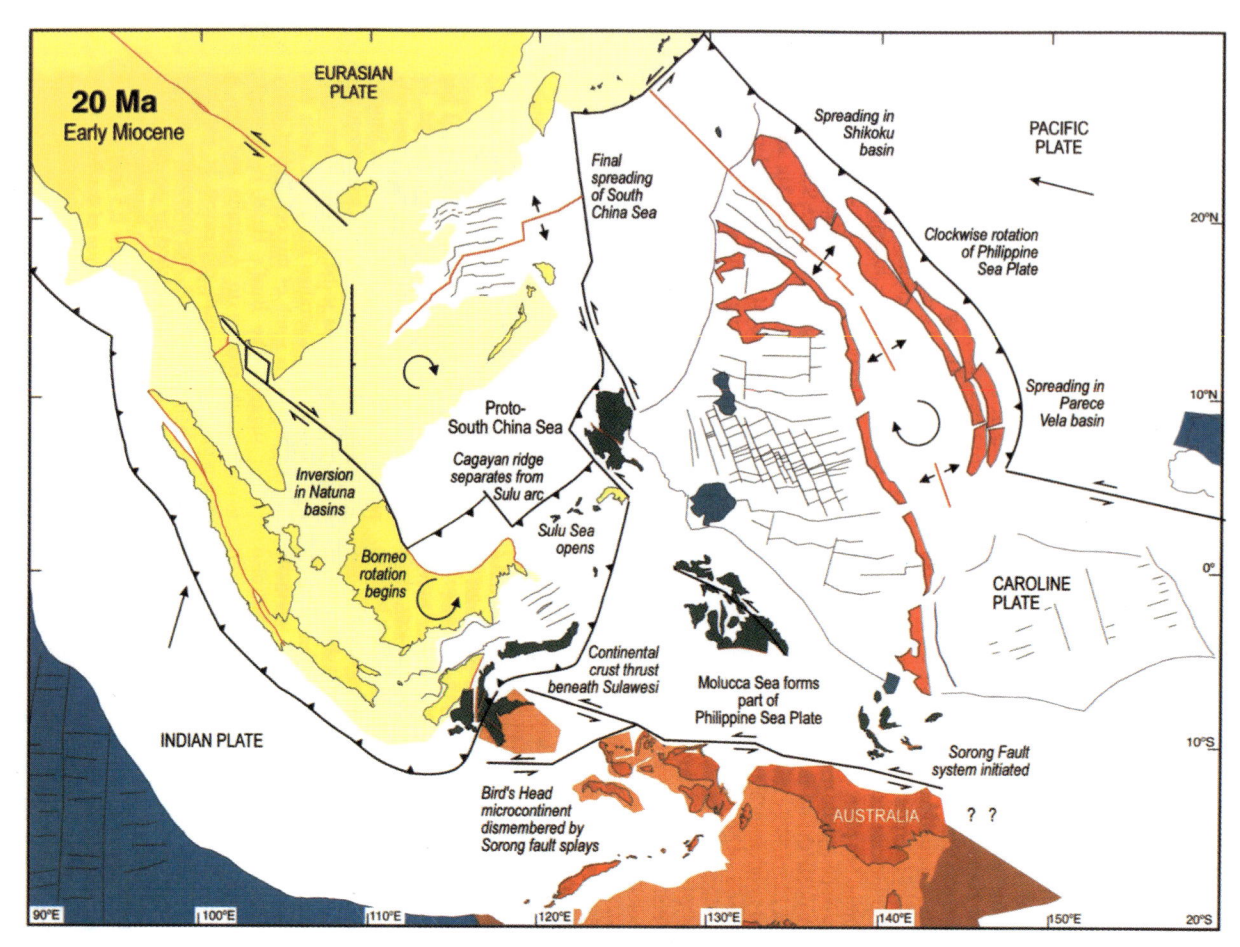

Figure I.18. Reconstruction of the region at 20 Ma. Rotation of Borneo and parts of Malaya, Sumatra and Java began. Subduction of the proto-South China Sea caused a split of the Sula arc and the separation of the active arc of the Cagayan ridge. The opening of the South China Sea propagated in a south-westerly direction onto the Sunda shelf *(Source: Tectonic Evolution of Southeast Asia, Geological Society Special Publication No. 106)*

years ago – see figure I.19) the rotation of the Malay Peninsula along the spliced Three Pagodas Fault system continued, and a pull-apart basin formed the Gulf of Thailand (figure I.20). This rotation process was completed 10 million years ago in the Late Miocene.

However the northern branch of the Three Pagodas Pass at Wang Chao remains active. Satellite remote sensing data show a clear trace for the fault system in the area North-West from Bangkok. From subsurface data it is known that the North-South trending fault shows a down-dip of over 1,000 m on the western side. This movement correlates with the regional perceived stress relations.

Earthquakes along the northwestern extension of the Three Pagodas Fault zone – the Sagaing fault – are severe. Bangkok is located near the intersection of the Three Pagodas Fault zone and the Chao Phraya Fault zone.

Historic evidence (Nutalaya, 1983) shows numerous slight tremors felt in Bangkok over the last 200 years, it is not known if they are related to movement of one of the 2 major fault zones.

Based on this historic evidence, the risk for earthquake damage appears quite small. However the structural setting, discussed above, with known activity along the Three Pagodas Fault zone in Myanmar suggests that further movements will certainly take place and may cause severe tremors in

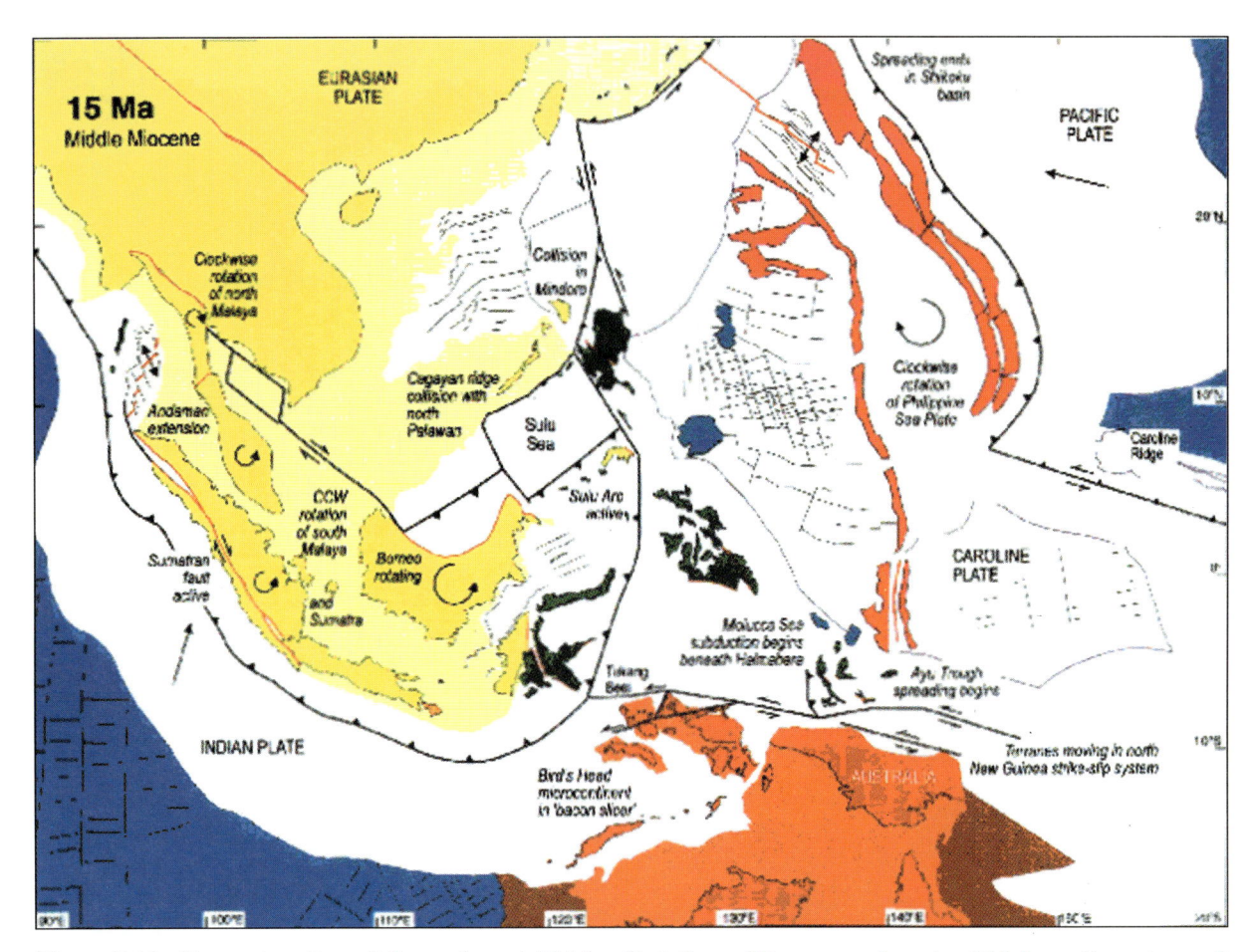

Figure I.19. Reconstruction of the region at 15 Ma. Rotation of Borneo and parts of Malaya, Sumatra and Java were under way. Strike-slip motion at the southern boundary of the Philippine Sea plate fragmented the Bird's Head microcontinent and moved blocks west in the plate boundary zone. Similar motions were occurring in the northern Philippines. The back-arc Sulu Sea began to close after collision of the Cagayan ridge with the Palawan margin *(Source: Tectonic Evolution of Southeast Asia, Geological Society Special Publication No. 106)*

the Bangkok region. The unconsolidated, water-rich sediments underlying the city may liquefy similarly to what happened in Kobe (1995) causing much surface damage. The Kobe earthquake is reported to relate to fault movement with a 2,000-year activity return time (Okumura, 1999).

(ii) Flooding and storms

The Bangkok metropolis is located in a subsiding basin at the mouth of the Chao Phraya River. The monsoon rainfall cumulates near the end of the rainy season, when the run-off from the West, Northwest and North reaches its maximum volume and heavy daily rainfall occurs. The multiple dams and large water reservoirs allow water management at a reasonable level, safeguarding Bangkok. The main risks occur when several tropical rainstorm depressions hit Thailand while dams upstream are already filled to capacity. In such cases, the river may burst its embankment and inundate large areas, as has happened frequently in the past before any human intervention.

If a major rain depression (typhoons do not normally affect Bangkok) hits Bangkok at the same time, pushing up the sea level, the magnitude of the disaster increases sharply.

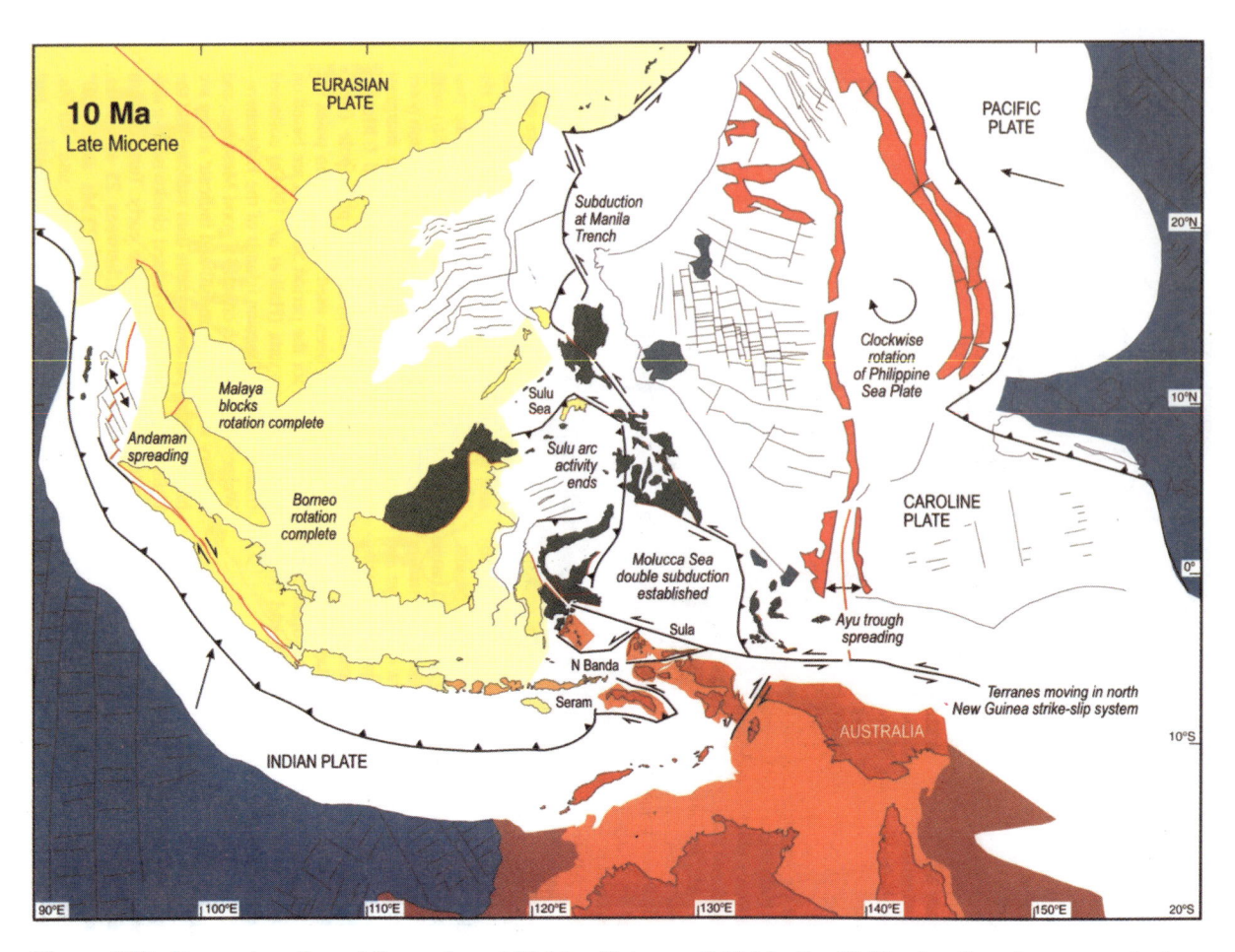

Figure I.20. Reconstruction of the region at 10 Ma. Between 5-25 Ma the Philippine Sea plate rotated about a pole at 15ºN, 160ºE. Counterclockwise rotation of Borneo and related rotations of Sundaland were complete *(Source: Tectonic Evolution of Southeast Asia, Geological Society Special Publication No. 106)*

(iii)   Sea level rise and basin subsidence

The Bangkok Basin is still subsiding. Previously, annual flooding would compensate for these phenomena, but with the current of system of levees – or dikes – containing the rivers, this no longer happens. It has been postulated by several scientists that sea levels are rising as a result of global warming.

As a large part of the city is near or just above current sea level, culmination of the above-mentioned events would cause serious problems. A complete polder system with many dikes would be required to keep the water out. Building and managing such a complex system will be extremely expensive. This geohazard poses a severe risk to Bangkok in the medium term.

G. Natural stone in cities

Humans have always used natural stone in their habitat. The huge agglomeration of people in urban settings has resulted in an ever-increasing demand for these materials. The following categories of application can be distinguished:

1. Exterior cladding for buildings
2. Interior use, mainly for flooring
3. Street pavements and decoration
4. Memorial stones

It is a well known fact in the world of natural stone that the amount spent on natural stone materials has increased continuously over the last few decades and now reaches 12 per cent of the costs of hard building materials. Considering the number of buildings in a metropolis, total expenditure for categories 1 and 2 is enormous.

All urban agglomerations develop the need for inner city shopping and entertainment areas. Also everywhere streets have to be dug up to work on the underlying infrastructure e.g. sewerage, water supply, power lines etc.

Figure I.21. Example of granite pavement properly selected and installed

Figure I.22. Granite cracking due to poor installation
and specifications of the selected stone

Natural stone pavement is commonly used because of its perceived beauty, but also of its cost effectiveness. Concrete and clay brick pavements are less durable, and each time they are dug up, a considerable proportion is damaged. For the same reason often natural stone kerbing is used instead of concrete, which is damaged more quickly by heavy trucks passing over them.

Decoration stone is used to enhance the setting of both inner city developments and landscaping. Government and private people are using it for these purposes.

Finally natural stone has always been used for funeral work. This varies from simple structures, tombstone to very complex entities such as for instance the Egyptian Pyramids.

In early development stages, all materials are sourced from nearby quarries. Transport cost of this heavy material is one of the main items restricting application. Once infrastructure becomes well established, transport cost is no longer prohibitive. Today materials are shipped in big volumes across the entire world.

Originally only local stone supply was used, so extensive know-how was established on the quality and building parameters. Now the application range has widened so much that this is no longer feasible. Testing of materials determines suitability, but as application stretches over a very long period mishaps occur frequently. Further many users are poorly informed on the stone parameters and the significance of those.

Application of natural stone in the categories 1, 2 and 3 depends on the nature of the stone and the setting where the stone is used. Several examples spring to mind to illustrate this. Cladding for high-rise buildings must be resistant to microclimatic conditions such as wind and stresses due to heating or cooling, pollution, vibrations, fungus etc.

Adequate building regulations and proper supervision is needed to ensure that safety norms are respected.

The conditions for flooring are less strict as the hazard effect is negligible. However the material used is expensive, so proper evaluation is required to ensure that no capital is wasted on remedying failures.

Pavement selection and installation need to be strictly monitored to safeguard against wrong material selection, and proper recognition of subsoil conditions and their influence on the planned work. Failures tend to be very costly.

The above-mentioned examples of natural stone application in an urban setting demonstrate the need for adequate geological know-how to safeguard the public against hazardous situations and capital waste.

H. Urban geology, costs and benefits

Urban agglomerations host large populations and represent very large investments. Each citizen pays its share in the development and maintenance, either directly or indirectly, of such a megapolis. It has been described here that management of cities without following the multi-disciplinary approach of geology for planning or urban geology will bring about costly disasters. All developments relate directly to the local and regional geological settings. Those form the foundation of the entire entity. Without a proper foundation no real guarantee can be given for future usage. Damages caused may affect individuals directly or the community at large.

Quantifying costs is a difficult matter. Published figures from the United Kingdom (Marker, 1996) show that 60 per cent of geotechnical expenses are for low-rise building foundations, and that close to 10 per cent of this amount is spent on remedial work. High costs are associated with damage caused by subsidence, leaks of the water and sewerage systems, damage to roads, bridges, etc.

An interesting assessment is given by ESCAP (1996), under Economic Factors and Cost/Benefit Analysis. Examples are quoted from the Netherlands, were damage claims, due to insufficient geological knowledge provided by the Government to contractors, were compared to the cost of collecting these geological data plus the extra costs to prevent these problem. A total of nine claims of 17.35 million guilders included in the study could have been avoided by geological surveys and the resulting remedial work totaling about 1.7 million. The costs of carrying out the necessary geological work plus the remedial work are therefore roughly 1 per cent of the amount claimed and spent. This figure gives an indication of the amounts and benefits involved. Another probably more significant example is provided (in the same article) for the city of Amsterdam. A set of urban geology maps was produced based on existing and newly collected data. This total cost is compared with the actual expenditure on executing works in the city and the savings realized by having those thematic maps available. It shows that the costs incurred are recovered in a period between 1 to 3 years.

It was also reported at the 3rd session of the ESCAP Forum on Urban Geology in Asia and the Pacific-cum-Project Review Meeting in Shanghai, 1997 by the participants from Shanghai-Pudong area that huge savings had been realized by implementing Urban Geology in their development plans. Savings realized by modifying the city design on lower foundation costs are estimated at 0.8-1 billion RMB Yuan (~US $100-125 million). Further by relocating the airport, savings of about 300 million RMB (~36 US $ million) were obtained.

Though not conclusive, those numbers demonstrate that urban geology is a relatively cheap planning tool and provides substantial benefits to the community at large as well as individuals.

The example quoted under B above from Hobart, Tasmania, Australia further underlines the misery and costs, which may result from failing to incorporate geological data in development and infrastructure projects.

In a city like Bangkok, reliable subsurface maps showing suitable piling horizons, subsidence rates and sedimentary structures would help to save substantial costs in the design and preparation of various projects such as buildings, roads, sewerage, water distribution and waste management.

Over the years, ESCAP spent about US $500,000 as seed money to promote the use of urban geoscience by all countries it serves. Several countries responded well and started their own independent work. As mentioned above, China carried out urban geology work in Shanghai which resulted in huge cost savings, illustrating the importance and cost-effectiveness of this particular ESCAP programme.

J. Managing data or saving money

Starting urban geology projects, the researcher may spend hours, weeks or even months locating, gathering, sorting and verifying the data needed. More and more researchers are spending huge amounts of time managing data instead of interpreting them. The barriers to the effective use of data can be described as an obstacle course.

Before interpretation work can begin many steps need to be performed, primarily manually and by the interpretor him- or herself. The required data may already be in-house, but may reside on tape, floppy disk or paper logs in some filing cabinet. Data management becomes a large part of the interpreter's job, easily taking most of the time, instead of being able to focus on interpreting the data.

Data formats can raise additional hurdles. Paper or digital records must be entered into the format of choice, then validated and possibly corrected. Whilst all this happens, interpreting has not yet to start and results are needed, deadlines approaching. There is a trade-off between doing it well and doing it quickly.

If finding data is the first hurdle, integrating information from different databases can be even more frustrating. Software problems often hamper information flows between various hardware systems. Development of interactive links between databases is one important step. With new technology, data management chores can be performed in the background with supervision by a technician or machines. This realignment allows data management to move out of the interpretation flow. Data comes and goes into a standard format, access as easy as getting electric power.

The alignment process requires five key elements:

- Vision
- Technology
- Processes and procedures
- Performance systems
- An action plan

Processes and procedures are the steps taken to implement the technology, i.e., how you can make changes and use the equipment. The performance system is an easy way to gauge performance, if you cannot measure the equipment and people performing, you cannot control them.

A five-step Data Management Maturity Model introduced by d'Angelo and Troy (2000) is shown here:

- Base
- Managed
- Corporate Competency
- Predictable Risk
- Fully Optimized

Base level depends largely on the talents of individuals, whose expertise may easily be lost, if he or she leaves the organization. At the other end of the scale everything is fully operated and the system is risk free. The costs escalate at each step of data management.

Operating at level 2, including standardized tasks and introduction of advanced technology, but demanding crucial individual expertise, seems best for urban geology's complex data management requirements.

Warehousing allows data to be stored after it has been verified and put into a readily accessible format. The productivity of the users increases sharply with the use of network attached warehouse storing. Proper storing of data and accessing the application off-site can allow the users to focus on their main tasks, rather than on the upkeep of data and software.

References

d'Angelo and Troy, 2000: Managing Data or Finding Oil, in Explorer, American Association of Petroleum Geologists, August 2000, pp. 26-27.

Bangkok Post, various editions, 1999 and 2000.

ESCAP, 1990a: State of the Environment in Asia and the Pacific in Asia and the Pacific 1990, United Nations, Bangkok.

ESCAP, 1990b: Geology for land-use planning in tropical delatas, Atlas of Urban Geology, volume 5, United Nations, Bangkok.

ESCAP, 1996: Manual on Environmental and Urban Geology of Fast-Growing Cities, Atlas of Urban Geology, volume 9, United Nations, New York.

European Commission, 1995: Europe's environment: Statistical compandium for the dobris assessment, Office for Official Publications of the European Communities, Luxembourg, 455 p.

European Environment Agency, 1995: Europe's environment: The Dobris assessment, Office for Official Publications of the European Communities, Luxembourg, 712 p.

Hall, R. and D.J. Blundell, editors, 1996: Tectonic Evolution of Southeast Asia, Geological Society of London Special Publication 106 (Royal Holloway, London University), London, 584 p.

Lea, J.P. and J.M. Courtney, 1986: "Cities in Conflict. Studies in Planning and Management of Asian Cities, World Bank, Washington.

Marker, B.R., 1996: Urban development: Identifying opportunities and dealing with problems, in Urban Geoscience, by McCall, G.J.H., E.F.J. De Mulder, B.R. Marker (eds.), Balkema, Rotterdam.

McCall, G.J.H., E.F.J. De Mulder, B.R. Marker (eds.), 1996: Urban Geoscience, Balkema, Rotterdam.

Okumura, Koji, 1999: Kobe earthquake of January 1995 and studies on active faulting in Japan, in Atlas of Urban Geology, volume 10, pp. 205-217, United Nations New York.

Symposium on Mineral, Energy and Water Resources of Thailand, Towards the Year 2000, Oct. 1999, Department of Geology, Chulalongkorn University, Bangkok, Thailand.

II. LAND SUBSIDENCE IN BANGKOK: AN OVERVIEW OF CHANGES DURING THE LAST 23 YEARS

by

Michiel Bontenbal[1]

A. Introduction

1. Land subsidence

The city of Bangkok, Thailand has been subjected to land subsidence, in the past as well as nowadays. Land subsidence can be defined as a gentle and continuous lowering of the ground surface, very often experienced in areas with a relatively soft soil. It is however worth noting that in the Bangkok area this subsidence has reached severe proportions. For example: in some areas a maximum subsidence of about one metre has been observed over the last 23 years (since the research started in 1978).

The consequences of such severe land subsidence are clear and can be divided into two categories:

- Damaging and destruction of the infrastructure such as the foundations of buildings, buried pipelines, wastewater sewers, roads and bridges
- Disturbing of the local water system, for instance extensive and more intense flooding by river or seawater, intrusion of salt water to the aquifers, disturbing and deterioration of the existing rainwater drainage system.

The phenomenon of land subsidence has been studied by others in the past and is quite well understood and documented. It can be said that subsidence can have both a natural and a human-induced cause. However, in most cases it is the result of a combination of the two. For the Bangkok area the main cause for subsidence is human-induced, viz., distraction of groundwater for drinking water purposes. This distraction lowers the pore pressure in the several sand and clay layers, resulting in a compression of these ground layers. The summation of the compression of the various layers is the total amount of land subsidence.

It should be noted that land subsidence is a general phenomenon that occurs in many areas of the world. Well-known case studies have been carried out for areas in California, Mexico City, Venice, the Mississippi Delta, Jakarta, Shanghai and The Netherlands.

2. Previous research in the Bangkok area

Cox (1968) first remarked on land subsidence. In the newspapers there was some attention to the problem in 1969. In the early seventies various researchers, mainly at the Asian Institute of Technology (AIT) carried out research on the problem.

In 1978, AIT, under the leadership of Prinya Nutalaya, started the first comprehensive research on land subsidence in the Bangkok Area. (AIT, 1981). It was found that the rate of subsidence was more than 10 cm/year. Under the leadership of AIT and financed by the National Environment Board,

---

[1] Geologist, Kromme Waal 33-f, Amsterdam 1011 BW, Netherlands.

27 benchmarks for determining land subsidence were installed in 1978. In 1985 the Royal Thai Survey Department installed an additional 14 benchmarks.

Rau and Nutalaya have studied the geology of the Central Plain of Thailand. They have made maps showing the thickness of the Bangkok Clay.

In 1985 the Groundwater Division of the Department of Mineral Resources started the Project: "Mitigation of Groundwater crisis and Land subsidence in the Bangkok Area (MGL)". During this project benchmarks and groundwater monitoring stations were installed and the heights of the piezometric levels of the three most important aquifers were monitored. This project, that is still ongoing, revealed more data on the local geology and hydrology.

Over the years a number of small research projects has been carried out by various researchers determining a better understanding of the geology, geomorphology, (geo-)ecology and hydrology of the Central Plain.

The Japanese International Cooperation Agency (JICA 1995, 1999) and the Netherlands Engineering Consultants (NEDECO 1987, 1996) carried out some major investigations about flood-protection and land subsidence.

It is worth noting that much research about the problem is published in Thai and therefore, unfortunately, inaccessible to the author.

3. Research project

In order to investigate the problem of land subsidence in the Bangkok area a limited literature study and data-interpretation project was carried out by the author at the office of the United Nations Economic and Social Commission for Asia and the Pacific (ESCAP) in Bangkok. In consultation with the Water and Mineral Resources Section (WMRS) the following objectives for this research project were drafted:

- Study the physical processes responsible for the subsidence and compare the spatial distribution of the subsidence with the thickness and extension of the geologic strata in the area.
- Map the spatial distribution of the subsidence over the years, using a Geographic Information System (GIS).
- Clarify the consequences of the subsidence and raise awareness among decision-makers and the general public.
- Compare the situation in Bangkok with other areas in the world where the subsidence problem also occurs and identify some areas in the Asian-Pacific region where it might occur in the future.

4. Internship programme

The research project was carried out by the author within the framework of his study at the faculty of Earth Sciences at the Vrije Universiteit (VU) Amsterdam, Netherlands. The report thus produced should be viewed as the equivalent to a Master of Science thesis in the Netherlands.

The work was carried out during an internship of three months at the office of UN ESCAP in Bangkok. It was conducted at the Water and Mineral Resources Section (WMRS) of the Environment and Natural Resources Development Division (ENRDD).

Mr. Huub van Wees, Economic Affairs Officer, WMRS was the author's mentor at ESCAP, while Prof. Pier Vellinga acted as mentor within the faculty of Earth Sciences at the Vrije Universiteit in Amsterdam, Netherlands.

The project lasted from November 8th 2000 until March 15th 2001. Consequently, the total time available for preparing this report was limited to 15 weeks. A final version of the report will be prepared at the faculty of Earth Sciences at the Vrije Universiteit Amsterdam, upon completion of the internship.

It is further worth noting that besides studying the subject and preparing this report, a substantial amount of time and effort went into the construction of a website on land subsidence. This page can be found at: *http://www.unescap.org/enrd/water_mineral/Land_main.htm*

5. Acknowledgements

A paper such as this could not have been prepared without the obliging accommodation and helpful assistance of many persons. Therefore the author wishes to thank the following persons and institutions.

UN ESCAP for the provided accommodation.

The Water and Mineral Resources Section, in particular Mr. H. van Wees, mentor, Mr. David Jezeph, Chief of the Section, Mr. Cihat Besocak, Mr. D. Jayawardena and former staff member Mr. Jon Rau for their support.

The Department of Mineral Resources, Ministry of Industry, for their help and gracious supply of data.

Ms. Somkid Buapeng of the Groundwater Division of the Department of Mineral Resources for the supply of data and literature on the subject.

Mr. Niran Chaimanee, Senior Geologist, Quaternary Geology Section, for help with the Quaternary geology of the Central Plain. Mr. Sin Sinsakul, Senior Geologist, Environmental Geology Section, for supplying pictures and other information. Mr. Sunya Sarapirome, Ph.D., Chief Geological Information Section, for assistance with a GIS-base map of the Central Plain.

Mr. Wolfgang Schirrmacher, Dr. Armin Margane, Dr. Jürgen Lietz and Dipl. Ing (FH) Klaus Mang of the Thai-German Technical Cooperation Project for support and technical information.

Mr. Surin Piyakulkunakorn, M.Sc. Student at the University of New South Wales, Sydney, Australia, for encouraging discussions on the subject.

Mr. Taco Hoencamp, IWACO, especially for introducing me to Mr. Panchote Kulvanit of Metrix Associates Co., LTD. Mr. Panchote Kulvanit and Ms. Kritika Trakoolngam at Metrix are acknowledged for their valuable support.

Mr. Ksemsan Suwarnarat, Deputy Director General of the City Planning Department, Bangkok Metropolitan Administration for lending valuable documentation.

Maarten Kuijper (IOC-WESTPAC, UNESCO), Han Westerwerp (Delft Hydraulics), Wil Borst (Netherlands Dredging Consultants), Frits Ariesen (ESCAP consultant) and Jorge Carrillo (ESCAP) for their support in various fields.

B. Description of the project area

1. Geology and hydrogeology of the Central Plain

(i) General geologic setting

The Central Plain of Thailand (also known as the Chao Phraya Plain) is located within a north-south trending structural depression, which was generated by fault block tectonics during the Late Pliocene – Pleistocene time. (Rau and Nutalaya, 1980). The depression was filled in with alluvial, fluvial, deltaic and shallow marine sediments during the Quaternary Period. The total thickness of the Quaternary sediments in the basin ranges from 400 to more than 1,800 m (ESCAP secretariat, 1988).

It can be stated that the hydrogeologic setting of the Central Plain is rather complex, with alternating sand and clay layers. The Department of Mineral Resources (DMR) has distinguished a total of eight aquifers.

See figure II.2 for the hydrogeologic North-South profile of the Lower Central Plain. Impermeable clay layers (or aquitards) separate the permeable sand layers (or aquifers). A description of the eight aquifers is given in table II.1.

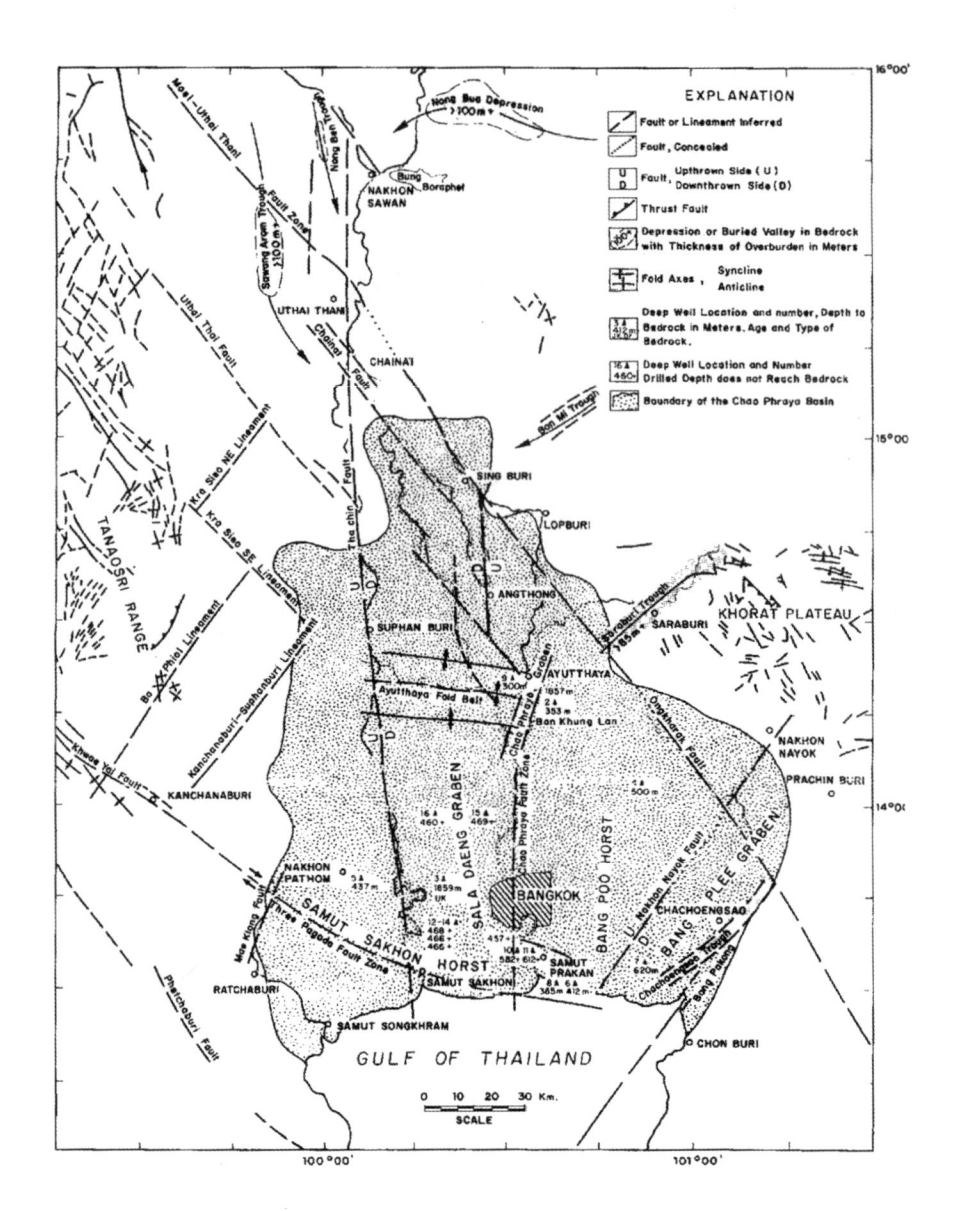

Figure II.1. Map of the structural basin of the Central Plain. The faults, depth of the
Quaternary sediments, locations of some deep drillings and the
main topographic features are represented on this map.
(ESCAP secretariat, 1988)

Later studies (Nguyen Anh Duc, Rau) revealed that the distribution of the strata is more complex than represented in figure II.2. The strata are not always continuing and there are clay and sand lenses in the sediments. So it must be clear that this subdivision of the geology of the Central Plain is an abstraction of the reality. The geology of young, marine and fluvial sediments is often complex and difficult to classify. The Holocene geology of the Netherlands is also a good example of this.

This has some important consequences for the geohydrology. At places where the clay layers are absent a direct hydraulic connection exists between adjacent aquifers. Since the lowering of the piezometric level of the aquifer is important for the total land subsidence, it is important to know and map the geological differences in the area to be studied.

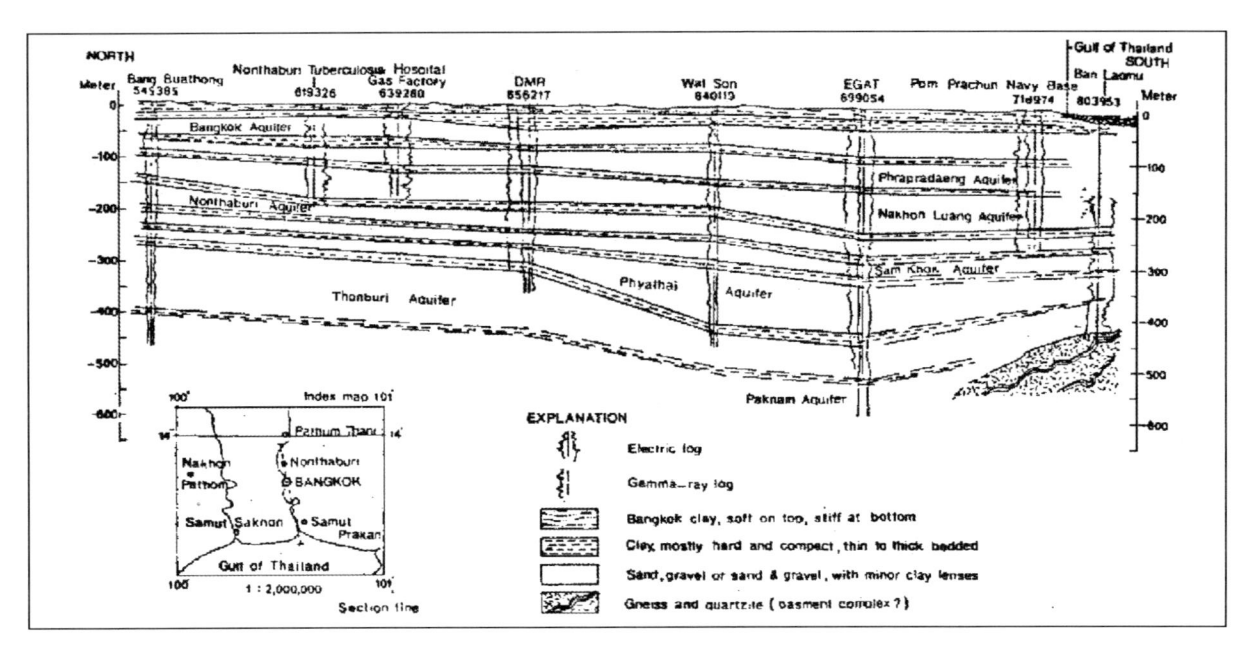

Figure II.2. Hydrogeologic north-south profile of the lower Central Plain showing the principal aquifers of the Bangkok Multi Aquifer System
(after Charoen Phincharoen & Somkid Buapeng, 1973)

(ii)   The Bangkok Clay

The Bangkok Clay was deposited during the Holocene Transgression, from 11.000-3.000 years BP. During that period the whole Central Plain was below sea level and was a tidal flat. The sea reached as far inland as Ayutthaya, approximately 90 km away from the current sea shore.

Rau and Nutalaya (1983) described the Bangkok Clay as a complex of two deposits, a basal stiff clay and an upper soft clay. The uppermost two metres is referred to as weathered clay.

a. *Stiff Bangkok Clay.*

- *Description*: This is a heterogeneous clay and the layer is interbedded with sand and silt. The thickness varies from circa 5 to 35 m. The clay is moderate brown to light-brown and yellowish brown (AIT, 1981). Red and yellow coloured mottles are present. Also some calcareous concretions (calcrete) are present in the clay.
- *Genesis*: The stiff clay is interpreted as a floodplain deposit following channel migration. The mottles indicate that the clay was exposed to sub-aerial processes.
- *Age*: The stiff Clay is dated by AIT (1981) and the age of the ten ^{14}C-samples ranges from 45,000 ± 6,900 to 14,700 ± 2,300 year BP. The sediments are deposited during the regression of the last Ice Age, when eustatic sea level was some 70-100 m below present.
- *Top:* The top of the stiff clay is a pronounced discomformity or erosion surface. A difference in colour is also visible.

b. *Soft Bangkok Clay.*

- *Description*: This homogeneous clay layer is generally 10 to 20 metres thick (in the Bangkok area) and is characterized by olive-gray and medium to dark-gray clay containing shell fragments and plant remains (Sinsakul, 2000).
- *Genesis*: The clay is marine and intertidal in origin.
- *Age*: Holocene: 11.000-3.000 years BP.
- *Top*: The top of the soft Bangkok Clay is the ground surface.

Table II.1. Description of the Bangkok multi aquifer system

Aquifer	Lithology	Water bearing Properties
1 Bangkok 50 m zone	Topmost clay is generally dark gray to black, limonitic lateritic in the upper portion. Coarse sand, gravel and pebbles are subangular to rounded, moderately well sorted; composed mostly of various types of fragments.	Yields considerable quantity of water of poor quality, brackish to salty and highly mineralized. Normally not developed as a groundwater resource.
2 Phra Pradaeng 100 m zone	Separated from the Bangkok aquifer by a dark stiff clay bed. Gravel-sand is characteristically white to pale gray, subrounded to rounded, fairly well sorted; composed mostly of quartz, chert and other rock fragments; with carbonised woods and peats in the lower part. Clay lenses interbedded in places.	Yields water of good quality only in the south and southwest of Bangkok; in other areas the aquifer yields brackish to salty water.
3 Nakhon Luang 150 m zone	Overlaid by thick and hard clay bed. Sand-gravel layers, which form the aquifer are rather thick (10-15 m). Fragments: mostly quartz, feldspar and quartzite; are sub-angular to subrounded, moderately to well sorted. Interbedding clays are whitish to yellowish to grayish brown, sandy and limonitic, non-plastic.	Has been heavily developed for public water supply. Yields 100-250 m^3/hr of excellent quality. Only in the south and southwest of Bangkok wells yield salty water due to salt water intrusion of the aquifer.
4 Nontha Buri 200 m zone	General characteristics of the formation are the same as the Nakhon Luang aquifer. It consists of rather uniform thick sands and gravel with minor sandy clay lenses. The formation can be divided into three units separated by leaky clay layers.	Is one of the most productive aquifers, which yields up to 200 m^3/hr of water of excellent quality. The water has been extensively used for bottled drinking water and brewerage as well as domestic supplies.
5 Sam Khok 300 m zone	The formation consists of sand, gravel and clay. Sand-gravel is yellowish brown to dirty brown, but may grade to white color, medium to very coarse grained, angular to sub-rounded, fairly well sorted, feldspars, calcareous due to limestone fragments in places; with interlacing clays. Both sand-gravel and clay beds are moderately to highly compact.	Yields slightly less than those of the Nakhon Luang and Nontha Buri aquifers. Normally penetrated by production wells in northern Bangkok since shallower aquifers yield water of higher iron content.
6 Phaya Thai 350 m zone	Consists of sand gravel and clay, Sand and gravel are dirty brown, angular, sizes range from medium to gravel, poorly to fairly well sorted; quartz and chert being major components. Clay is brown to dark brown, compact, calcareous and lateritic.	Wells drilled in central and southern Bangkok yield brackish to salty water while those in northern Bangkok produce fresh water. The aquifer is not popular due to its greater depth.
7 Thon Buri 450 m zone	Separated from the upper formation by hard and compact clay. Sand and gravel beds are usually alternated layering with clay beds. Color is generally gray to brownish gray to occasional white sand layers.	No production wells ever constructed, but the packer tests of several test holes indicate that the water is fresh to slightly brackish or mineralized in places. The aquifer is not so productive as the above aquifers due to the presence of clay in many horizons.
8 Pak Nam 550 m zone	Separated from the upper formation by leaky clay to sandy clay layer. Sand and gravel beds, generally thicker than that of the Thon Buri aquifer, are white to gray and well sorted. The clay is generally very compact, olive gray to dark gray, with carbonaceous matters.	The aquifer is very permeable and yields a considerable quantity of water of good quality. Water temperature is as high as 43°C. It is, however, too deep to reach by domestic wells, except in areas where there is no alternative potential aquifer; i.e. southern Bangkok.

There are, of course, lateral geological differences of the Soft Bangkok Clay. Rau & Nutalaya report that the rim of the Soft Bangkok Clay is marked at the western, northern and eastern side by a former beach-environment. The beaches are marked by fine-grained sand. This beach is the indicator for a still stand of sea level, because the beach needed sufficient time to develop.

This beach marks the high sea stand of the Holocene Climate Optimum (about 5,000 y BP) at about 5 metres above present sea level.

c. Weathered Clay

In various literature concerning the subject, especially in the geotechnical books, there is also mentioned a so-called "Weathered clay". Genetically the weathered clay is the same as the soft Bangkok Clay, but the distinction here is made on the geotechnical properties of the clay. Due to desiccation and cementation the weathered clay has different properties with respect to possible compaction (AIT, 1981). This will be further outlined below under C.

d. Fluvial sediments

The top layer, only the upper decimetres or so, consists of fluvial sediments, deposited after the regression in the Late Holocene. No special subdivision is made in the existing literature between marine and fluvial sediments in the Central Plain, because the fluvial sediments are too thin. These sediments consist mainly of clay and silt and were deposited during floodings. Floodings, in general, bring not only water but also fine particle sediment. Each year, until man built flood protection, the flood plain of the Chao Phraya River must have accreted vertically due to this sedimentation. Now, with the embankment of the river and the construction of several dams upstream, relatively little sediment is deposited during floods.

(iii) Spatial variation in thickness of the Bangkok Clay

The spatial variation of the thickness of the Bangkok Clay is important, because it gives an expectation for the total land subsidence. To this end these clays (soft, stiff) have been mapped by various institutes. A relevant map that has been produced by AIT (1981) is shown in figure II.3. The map shows the isopachs (i.e. lines with equal thickness) of the soft Bangkok Clay.

The thickness of the total Bangkok Clay has been investigated during the Mitigation of Groundwater crises and Land subsidence (MGL-project) whereby 98 corings were made. Unfortunately, in the description of the corings no subdivision was made between the soft and the stiff clay.

From the corings a map (figure II.4) with the total thickness of the Bangkok Clay (without distinction of soft and stiff clay) is produced (this study). The maps shows clearly the old drainage pattern, with in the middle of the map the buried valley of the palaeo-Chao Phraya River.

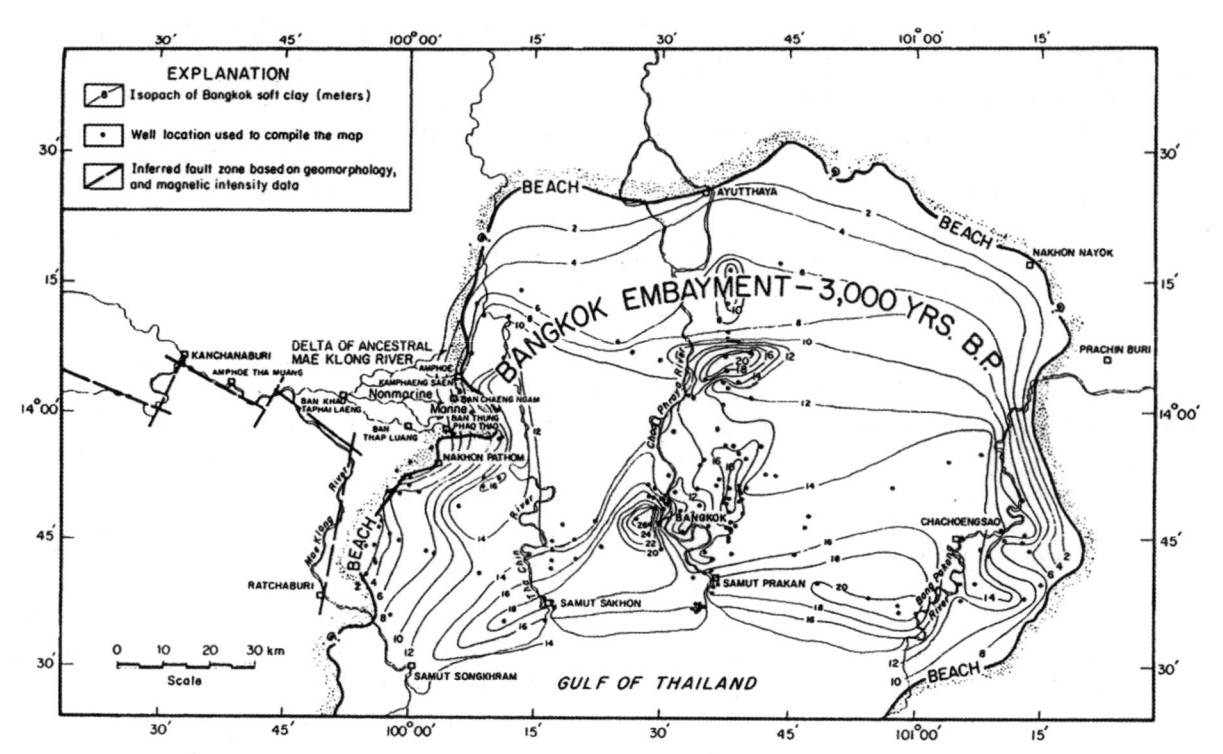

Figure II.3. Map of the Lower Central Plain showing the extension and thickness of the Holocene Soft Clay. Locations of the corings are also shown. *(AIT, 1981)*

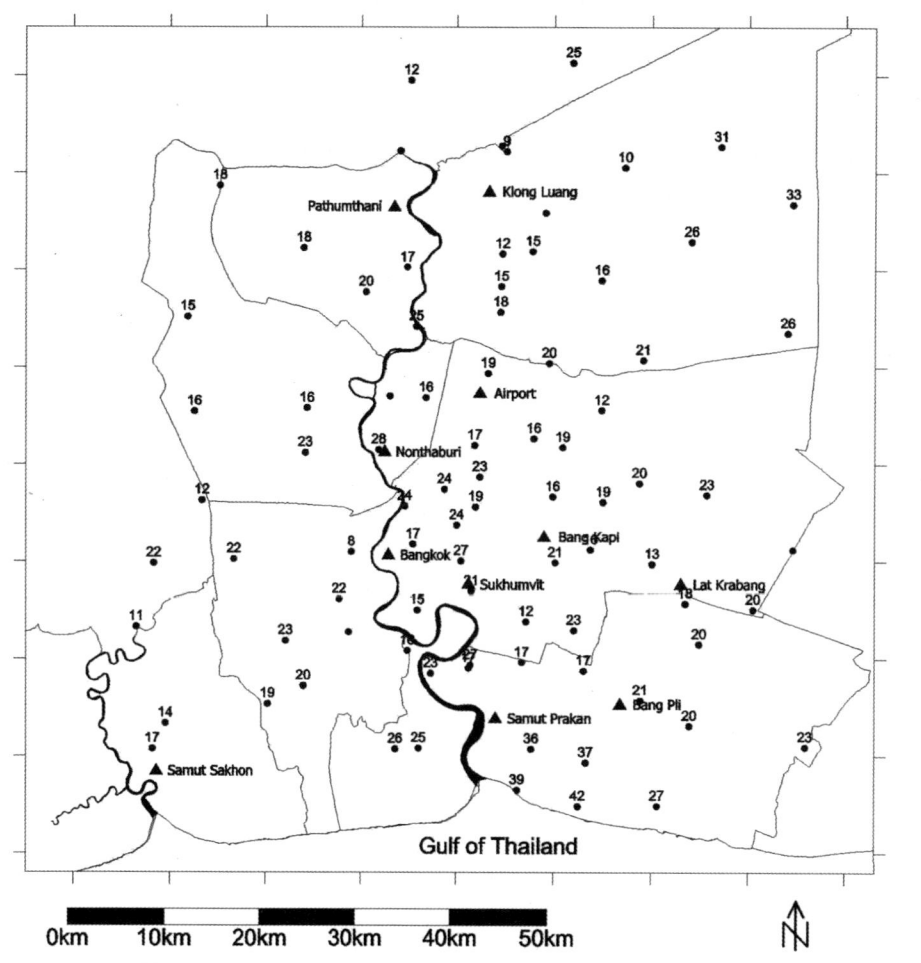

Figure II.4. Map with the thickness of the Bangkok Clay

2. Climate, water levels and tide

(i)   Climate of the Central Plain

   a.   General

The climate in the Central Plain is sub-tropical. In the extensively used Köppen-system it is classified as tropical and dry in the winter-season (so called *Aw*-classification). The climate is dominated by monsoons. In the winter (November-March) there is the dry, cool Northeast Monsoon. April to June is the hot, dry season, without a dominating monsoon. From July to October the wet Southwest Monsoon dominates the weather.

   b.   Precipitation

The annual precipitation in Bangkok is about 1,443 mm. The annual rainfall in the Bangkok Metropolis is higher than in the rest of the Central Plain, due to higher temperatures in the city (so-called "urban heat islands"). The annual precipitation in the rest of the Central Plain is about 1,200 mm.

To the east of the Central Plain the precipitation is even higher at 1,996 mm annually (JICA, 1995). This is caused by push rains up the Khorat Plateau.

Table II.2. Rainfall characteristics *(after NEDECO, 1987)*

Rainfall station	Bangkok Metropolis		Central Plain	
Frequency	1:2 year	1:5 year	1:2 year	1:5 year
1-day rainfall*	92	121	78	101
3-days rainfall	140	190	117	149
Annual rainfall	1 443	1 726	1 197	1 530

* In 24 hrs

From table II.2 it can be noted that the intensity of the rainfall can be quite high. Not particular the total annual precipitation but the intensity and duration (a few hours to three days) of the rainfall are the main causes of potential flooding. Especially when the Southwest Monsoon dominates weather the rainfall can be high. The Southwest Monsoon brings 86 per cent of the total annual precipitation (NEDECO, 1987).

   c.   Tropical Storms

Approximately two tropical storms per year occur, usually in the period from May to December (JICA, 1995). Generally speaking, Bangkok is outside the area where typhoons occur. Nevertheless, there is a frequency of once in thirty years that a typhoon presents itself in the area.

   d.   Evaporation

The estimated annual evaporation in the Bangkok area is about 1,800 mm (JICA, 1995). This means that the annual evaporation is larger than the annual precipitation.

(ii)   Chao Phraya River

The Chao Phraya River is Thailand's main river. Its total catchment area is about 160,000 km^2. In the river and its tributaries some dams are built, mainly to create basins for irrigation water. Upstream of the large Chao Phraya Dam (in Chainat Province) the discharge at present is 683 m^3/s. About 100 km downstream of this dam, near Ayutthaya, the discharge has decreased to 336 m^3/s

(JICA, 1995). It is noteworthy that calculations have revealed that during the high floods of 1942, before any dam in the river was built, a peak discharge of 4,000 m³/s has occurred (NEDECO, 1987).

The lower part of Chao Phraya River is in open connection with the Gulf of Thailand. Tidal influence can be measured up to 74 km from the river mouth. In the Lower Central Plain the river behaves as a meandering one.

(iii)   Tide and sea level in the Gulf of Thailand

Sea level varies in the Gulf of Thailand with the changing of the tides and with the changing of the monsoons. From November to January Mean Sea Level (MSL) is at its maximum and from June to July MSL is at its annual minimum. Also the tides are at their maximum from November to January. (NEDECO, 1987)

The tidal amplitude (difference between high water and low water) in the Gulf of Thailand is about 3.5 metres. During spring tides, the maximum sea level will reach about 1.7 m above mean sea level.

High tides may cause a so-called back-up effect when river discharges are high. This implies that the flow of river water will be blocked by the high tide, resulting in an even higher water level in the Chao Phraya River. Very often the river will than overflow its levees and dykes and will flood the surrounding land.

3. Anthropogenic factors

(i)   Growth of Bangkok

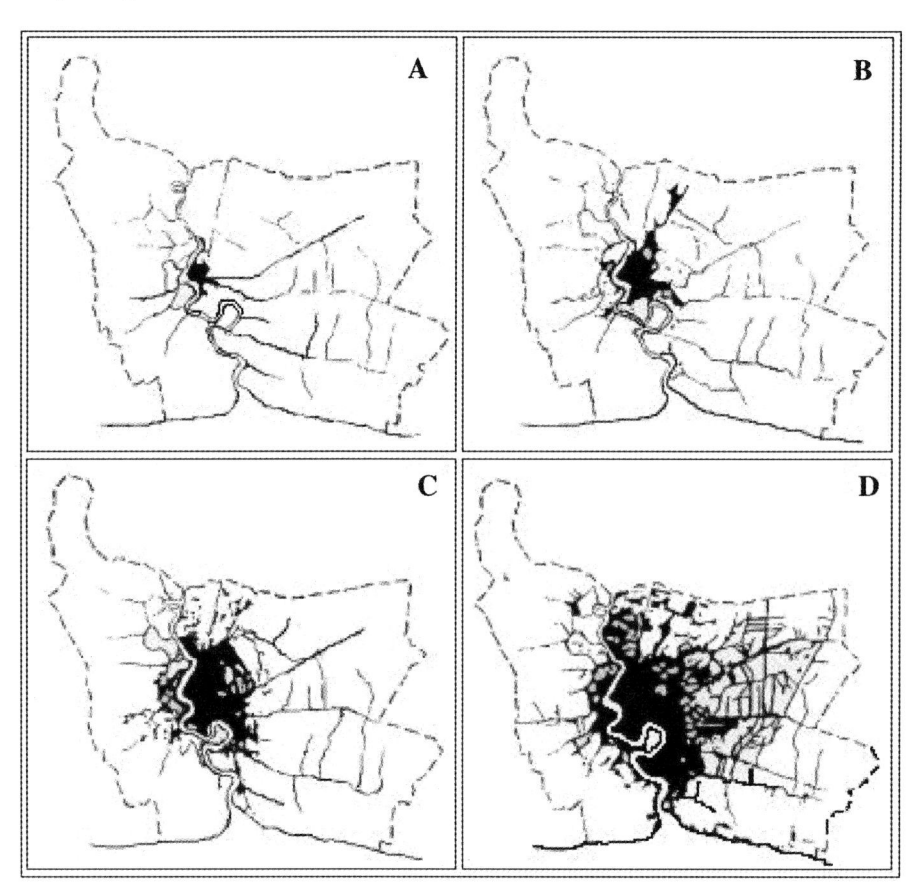

Figure II.5. Expansion of Bangkok over the years
A: 1900, B: 1958, C: 1974 , D: 1984 *(after ESCAP secretariat, 1988)*

Founded in 1782 as Thailand's new capital, in the first years of its existence Bangkok was only a small city. It was after World War II that the ongoing expansion of the city began. Especially during the Viet Nam War there was a large influx of capital to Bangkok, which in turn led to a huge increase in industrial activities and population. In 1974 the total population was about 4.1 million. By 1984 the population had increased to about 5.7 million. Also during the mid-1990s there was again a huge economical and construction boom, during which the population increased strongly. At the moment Bangkok is still expanding and growing, but the author knows no rates.

At present the population of Bangkok is 6.3 million officially. However, estimations made by the Bangkok Metropolitan Authority suggest that the real population of the Bangkok area is about 10 million.

(ii)   Canals in Bangkok

Since the founding of the city many canals (klongs) were dug with the aim to serve for transportation of goods and persons. Furthermore, some moats were dug to protect the new capital against foreign attacks. All together more than one hundred klongs and waterways were created in the early days of the town. The canal banks were lined with homes and shop houses, while the canals served as the 'highways' of their time. Tidal action flushed the river and klongs, thereby keeping them clean from sewage effluents.

At present, the klongs still serve as an open sewage and drainage system. Very often they have to cope with the torrential rains that can occur during the Southwest Monsoon. However, in the present days many klongs are filled in, in order to create new roads. Other klongs are not connected to the tidal action any more. This has the disadvantages that these open klongs, which are often used for dumping garbage and litter, will become clogged.

4. Water use in the Central Plain

(i)   Total water use and water supply in the Central Plain

Bangkok is a city that has a relative high water consumption per person per day. For this consumption two sources are available: treated surface water and groundwater.

a.   Treated surface water

The Metropolitan Water Authority (MWA) of Bangkok is responsible for the supply of drinking water and industry water to the citizens and industries. At present, the MWA produces mainly treated surface water. Over 99 per cent of the 4.5 million m^3/day provided by MWA are treated surface water. Approximately 91 per cent of this originates from the Chao Phraya River (Phuaprasert, 1998). The MWA further expects a growing demand of water of 0.2 million m^3/day every year.

Outside the area covered by the MWA the Provincial Waterworks Authorities (PWA) is responsible for the supply of water to the domestic users and industries. The PWA also mainly provides treated surface water to its users, but no exact information about this is available to the author.

b.   Groundwater

The other source of water for the city of Bangkok, groundwater pumped mainly by large industry users, accounts for an estimated 1.9 million m^3/day (DMR, 1998). For these large industries groundwater of their own well is cheaper than using treated surface water provided by MWA or PWA. More information on the pumping of groundwater is presented in paragraph *(ii)*.

c. Bangkok's total water consumption

The summation of the two water sources, treated surface water and groundwater, exceeds the 6 million m^3/day. With a maximum estimated population of Bangkok of some 10 million persons, the water consumption is more than 500 litres per person per day. As a comparison, Western Europe and the United States have an estimated water consumption of 100 to 200 litres per person a day.

Recently, MWA has set up an extensive demand side management programme to curb the water use by domestic users (Phraprasert, 1998).

(ii)   Legal and organizational aspects of groundwater use

It is very difficult, if not impossible, to estimate the total pumpage of groundwater in the Bangkok area and its surroundings. This is because the fact that besides the two earlier mentioned water distribution networks (MWA and PWA), groundwater is also exploited for domestic purposes. Four government agencies, namely, the office of Accelerated Rural Development (ARD), the Public Works Department (PWD), the Department of Mineral Resources (DMR) and the Department of Health (DOH) are involved in well constructions for the use of groundwater in those areas.

In general two types of wells exist:

- Public wells used by governmental institutions such as the city government, provincial governments and ministries. Public wells are generally not registered at the DMR. The institutes are required to measure their water use and then report this to the DMR.
- Private wells used by companies and domestic users. These wells have to be registered at the Groundwater Survey Division of the DMR. However, the DMR estimates that about 25 per cent of the total groundwater pumpage are unlicensed (Ramnarong and Buapeng, 1992). It is estimated that more than 10,000 private deep-water wells exist in the area. (JICA, 1995).

We should mention that companies or individual persons can get a license from DMR to pump groundwater for a period of ten years. During these years the license holder can pump without restrictions and consequently there is little control on the total amount of water that is pumped. After the ten-year period, the well can either be abandoned or remain in use. Without the control by DMR it is difficult to assess the total groundwater pumpage. In 1992, however, DMR had 1200 water meters installed in order to measure the actual water pumpage. It was observed that the amount of groundwater used by licensed users was some 25 per cent lower then permitted by the licenses. Nevertheless, this amount may be compensated by the unlicensed use of groundwater (Ramnarong and Buapeng, 1992).

a.   Pricing of the water

At present, little incentive is given to the industry to use treated surface water. Pumped groundwater is still cheaper for the industry than treated surface water. Industry price for a cubic metre of groundwater is currently about 4.5 baht (US $0.10) versus about 7 baht (US $0.15) for a cubic metre of treated surface water provided by the MWA.

(iii)   Amount of groundwater pumpage

a.   Public groundwater pumpage

Large-scale groundwater pumpage by MWA began in 1954 with a daily pumpage of 8,360 m^3/day. It more or less gradually increased until 1982 to a total pumpage of 440,000 m^3/day. After 1982 the groundwater pumpage by the MWA decreased, due to the new water supply policies: groundwater was replaced by treated surface water, following a Cabinet's resolution. In the 1990s, however, the groundwater use increased again due to the economic and construction boom.

b. Private groundwater pumpage

Before 1959 no data are available for pumping of groundwater by the private sector. Until 1975 the groundwater pumpage was relatively low, less than 0.6 million m^3/day. Between 1975 and 1982 the total groundwater pumpage more than doubled to 1.4 million m^3/day.

Due to control measures (as issued by a Cabinet's resolution) the groundwater pumpage decreased between 1983 and 1987. Between 1987 and 1996 groundwater pumpage has fluctuated, but since 1996 groundwater pumpage is increasing again.

c. Expansion of the city and water use

During city expansion, especially occurring in times of economic growth, the water supply in the new neighbourhoods depends entirely on groundwater pumpage. This is because no good surface water was available in those areas at the time. There was neither an adequate pipeline system nor a water-treatment plant that can provide treated surface water. Therefore the rate of pumped groundwater in those areas is higher than that in other areas. This extra pumping of groundwater will have an effect, as discussed hereafter, on land subsidence.

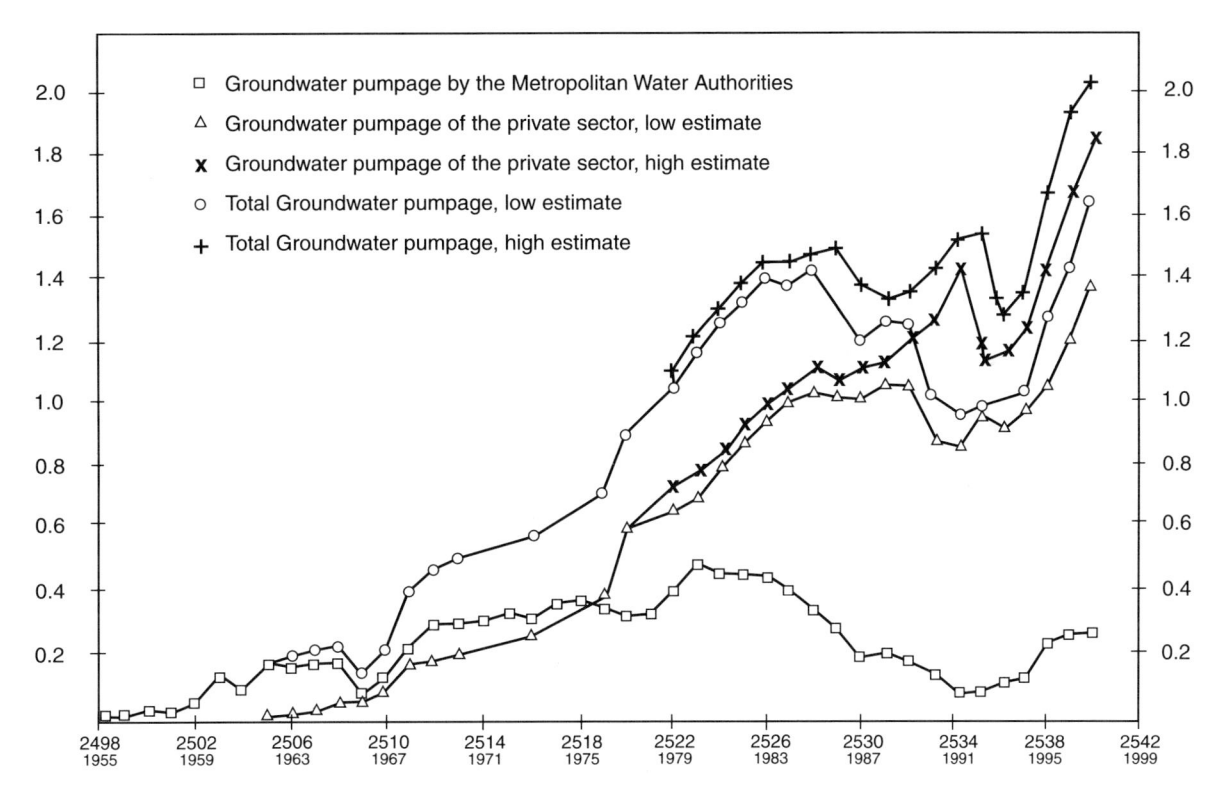

Figure II.6. Groundwater pumpage in the Bangkok area since 1955,
in millions of cubic metres per day (CMD, vertical axis);
on the horizontal axis the year as, top: BE, below: AD
(modified from DMR, 1998)

(iv)   Hydrological aspects of groundwater pumpage

a. Aquifer pumpage:

As described in paragraph *(i)* and table II.1 not all the eight aquifers in the Bangkok area are currently in use. The aquifers numbers 1 and 2 (Bangkok and Phra Pradaeng aquifers) were used for groundwater pumpage until they became too saline. These two aquifers were abandoned and numbers 3 and 4 (Nakhon Luang and Nontha Buri aquifers) were used for groundwater distraction. At the moment groundwater is mainly distracted from those two aquifers. (Ramnarong and Buapeng, 1992). However, no exact data are available on the amount of groundwater that is extracted from those two aquifers at the moment.

b. *The effects of groundwater pumpage on the piezometric level*

Due to the over-use of groundwater, the piezometric level in the aquifers of the Central Plain has lowered. Since the natural recharge of the aquifers is lower than the total pumpage, the aquifers become more and more depleted and the water level in the aquifers drops.

As a result of the lower water level, the pore water pressure will also drop. This lower pressure is one of the main causes of the land subsidence and will be further explained under C.

c. *Natural groundwater recharge:*

The water extracted from the aquifers is normally recharged in a natural way, e.g., by groundwater flow from other areas. However, such a natural groundwater recharge is limited because of slow flow of groundwater. The estimated sustainable yield for the total pumping in all the aquifers in the Bangkok area is estimated at 600,000 m^3/day (AIT and DMR, 1982). This means that 600,000 m^3/day can be pumped out and that this amount will be recharged via groundwater from other areas. Hence, a pumping rate above this level shall lead to a decline in piezometric level.

Due to the clay layers almost no percolation of surface water or precipitation occurs. AIT (1981) investigated that only 3 per cent of the groundwater is from direct percolation from soil layers and surface water. This implies that almost all pumped groundwater has to be recharged by groundwater flow.

Chuamthaisong and Yuthamanop (1980) studied the age and the isotopic composition of the groundwater in the Central Plain aquifers. They have found that the age varied from recent to ca. 20,000 BP. In the centre of the Central Plain Basin the water is old, near the boundaries of the basin the water is relatively young.

Because of this age variation Chuamthaisong and Yuthamanop (1980) concluded that it takes some 12,000 years for the groundwater to migrate from the boundaries of the basin to the centre (Bangkok). The natural recharge rate is slow; the two authors have calculated a speed of some 50 mm/day.

5. Historical overview of the situation in Bangkok

To get a good overview of the situation in Bangkok, it is important to get an overview of the researches that were done and measures taken to curb land subsidence.

In table II.3 a chronologic overview of events, researches and measures is presented. This overview is a good reference to occurrences and is necessary to establish a relationship between measures to curb land subsidence and the impacts it had on land subsidence.

Since the early 1990s neither important measures were taken to curb land subsidence nor were any new research projects started.

Table II.3. Chronology of events, researches and remedial measures taken to curb land subsidence

1930	First ground surface leveling in Bangkok by RTSD
1954	Start of large scale groundwater pumping
1965	Start investigation of groundwater resources of Bangkok by DMR
1967	First observation of salt groundwater in the aquifers
1969	First attention to land subsidence in the newspapers
1978-1982	Government supported comprehensive investigation programme
1978	Start measuring land subsidence, resurvey AIT/RTSD
1981-1985	Data gap, no geodetic levelings were carried out in this period
1983	◆ Major floodings in Bangkok ◆ Cabinet's resolution on groundwater pumping (issued in March) ◆ Implementation of Remedial Measures
1985	Start MGL-project. (Mitigation of Groundwater crisis and Land subsidence in Bangkok Metropolitan Area) Introduction of the groundwater charge on private users
1990-1991	Installation of benchmarks by the DMR for MGL-project

C. Land subsidence

1. Introduction

In this chapter the processes responsible for land subsidence will be explained. The rate and the spatial distribution of land subsidence will also be presented in the form of charts and maps.

Land subsidence, that is the gentle lowering of the ground, is a combination of natural and human-induced processes. Land subsidence occurs in many areas of the world, mainly in areas with a soft soil geology. There the geology consists of young unconsolidated material deposited in alluvial, lacustrine and/or shallow marine environments. Because of their unconsolidated nature, geologic layers are susceptible to land subsidence processes as compression and consolidation. In these areas many of the world's largest cities are built (e.g. Manila, Jakarta, Mexico City, New Orleans, Shanghai, Tokyo and the San Francisco Bay Area).

Land subsidence is a combination of both natural and human-induced geotechnical processes and is widely understood. The complex factors of geology, geotechnics, geohydrology and others make it a rather difficult problem to tackle in most areas. Several geotechnical equations (e.g. Terzaghi, full-coupling) can be used to calculate the subsidence.

2. Causes and geotechnical processes

(i)   Land subsidence mechanisms

The process of land subsidence is a complex phenomenon that can have multiple causes. However in most areas total land subsidence is a combination of two or more causes.

Poland and Davis (1956) defined 9 causes of land subsidence.

1. loading of the land surface
2. decline of artesian pressure in water sands
3. compaction or consolidation due to groundwater withdrawal
4. vibrations at or near the land surface
5. drying and shrinkage of deposits
6. oxidation of organic materials

7. tectonic movements
8. decline of pressure in oil zones due to the removal of hydrocarbons
9. solution due to groundwater withdrawal

It must be noted, however, that the broad range of names given to describe processes responsible for land subsidence is blurring the literature. Consolidation, compaction, settlement, compression, shrinkage, drying, self-weight loading are terms mentioned in the literature describing processes with the same effect: reduction of the vertical thickness of a particular geologic layer.

(ii)   Geotechnical methods used to calculate land subsidence

Although geology and geotechnics might seem, to laymen, a more or less similar field of research, their way of conducting research is quite different. Technical terms can have a different meaning in geology as in geotechnics.

Several of the above-mentioned geotechnical processes are responsible for the total land subsidence in the Central Plain. The two most important are compression of sand layers and consolidation of clay layers. Both processes are caused by a decrease in water pressure between the particles.

Geotechnically, the geological strata can be grouped in two major types:

- Aquifer: Coarse grained sediments (sands) with high permeability and low compressibility. The aquifers bear the groundwater.
- Aquitard Fine-grained sediments (clays, silts) with little permeability and relatively high compressibility. The aquitards bear almost no groundwater.

   a.   Consolidation or compaction

Consolidation, also known as compaction, is the process of load transfer to the soil as pore water escapes. This process occurs in the clay layers. The decrease in water pressure is due to the pressing out of the water by loading (i.e. the weight of buildings, roads) and to a decrease in water pressure in the surrounding sand layers.

Consolidation is a natural phenomenon that occurs in all clays, as a result of the weight of the sediments themselves. Construction of houses and roads enhances the rate of consolidation, through loading of the surface. Consolidation is an irreversible process.

Another process, closely related to consolidation, is known as shrinkage. It is a reversible process that is the result of dehydration of the soil due to evaporation. It occurs in the upper clay layers.

It is this particular response action (pore water depletion in the aquitard) that causes the subsidence observed at the ground surface – since water flow from the aquitard causes the consolidation of the aquitard.

   b.   Compression

Compression is the process of decreasing volume due to decreases in void spaces between the particles, occurring in sand layers. The void spaces can decrease because of the decline of water pressure in the aquifers. If the pressure decreases, the sand grains become more densely packed. Compression will be high when sands are initially loosely packed.

The process of total compression is very difficult to calculate or estimate when clay and sand layers are alternating on a small scale. The clay will fill in the voids between the sand particles, increasing the total compression. The sediments in the Central Plain (tidal, deltaic and fluvial in origin) show a high lateral and vertical variation, often resulting in sands alternating with clays. This is another reason why the (geotechnical) process of land subsidence is so difficult to tackle.

c. Overpumping of groundwater

In the early stage of pumping most water is drawn from the aquifers. This results in a lower piezometric level in this aquifer, developing a hydraulic gradient between aquifer and aquitard. This hydraulic gradient induces flow from the aquitard to the aquifer accompanied by a decrease in hydraulic head of the aquitard. Such a dewatering process of aquifer and aquitard leads to concurrent reduction in pore pressure, thus in pore volume and thus in land subsidence.

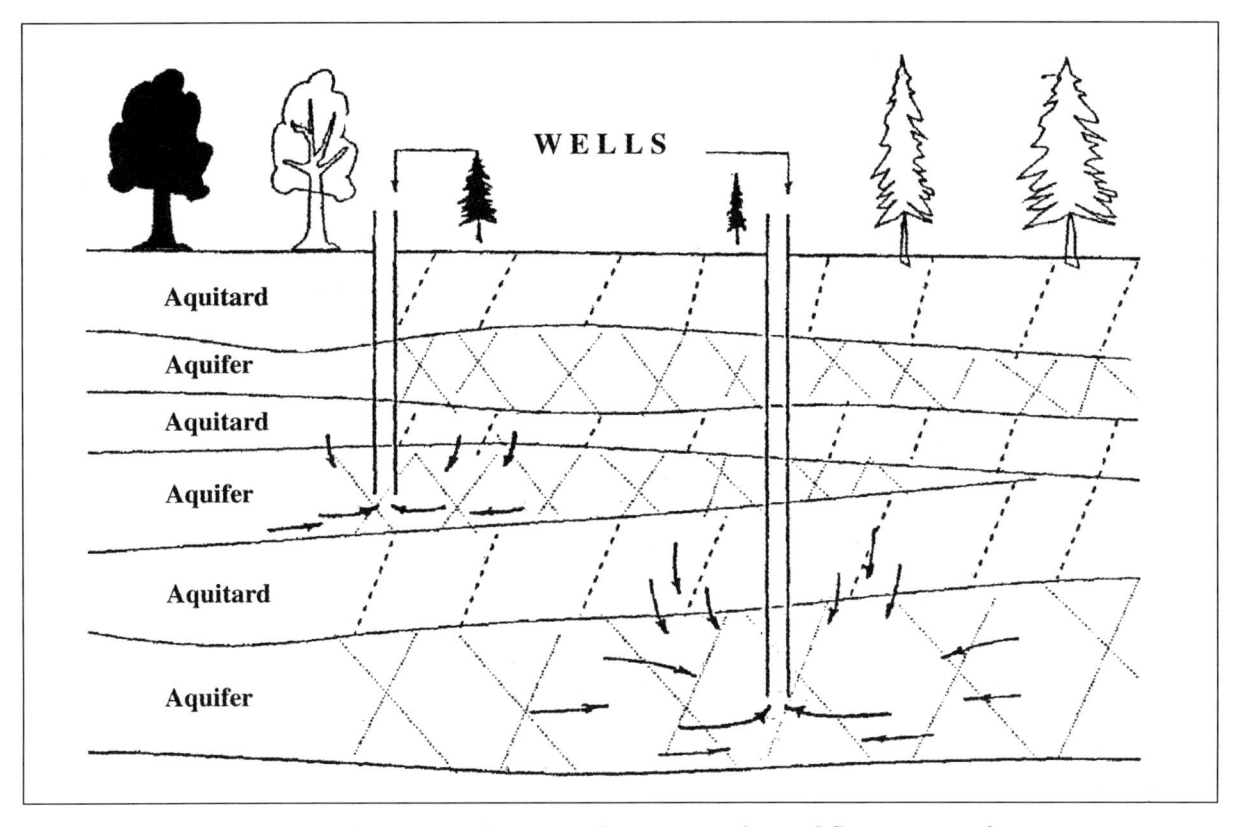

Figure II.7. Sketch showing groundwater pumping and flow response from a multi-aquifer/aquitard system
(after Yong et al., 1991)

In the geotechnical literature several formulas are given to calculate the compression and compaction (e.g. Terzaghi, full coupling). It is beyond the scope of this report to describe and analyze the best method and formulas used for calculating land subsidence, but some important parameters will be mentioned here.

d. Compression Index

The most important parameter for land subsidence is the Compression Index (C_c). Terzaghi (1943) defines it as the slope on a void ratio versus the log of pressure plot. The Compression Index is a dimensionless number. The Compression Index is a measure for the maximum possible consolidation of the soil layer to occur. If the Compression Index is high, the consolidation is expected to be high. If the Compression Index is low, the consolidation of that layer is expected to be low. When the Compression Index is negative, the sediment has been subject to preloading. This could be the case when sediments were buried and the overlying sediments have been eroded.

Table II.4. Compression indices for tested deltaic facies in the Mississippi Delta

Facies Unit	C_c Value
Peaty facies	4.72
Prodelta mud facies	1.03 – 2.25
Bay mud facies	0.82
Distributary mouth bar facies	0.12 – 0.23
Natural levee facies	0.12
Point bar sand facies	0.06
Beach sand facies	0.05

Kuecher (1995) has tested compression indices for different deltaic facies of the Mississippi Delta. The results of these tests are in table II.4.

It is clear from the table that the units that consist mainly of clay have a much higher compression index than the sandy units. The range of compression indices between facies types is great and far outweighs the variability of values within the same facies types. Furthermore, there is a trend that the finer the grainsize and the more distal a facies is, the larger the C_c value. This is most probably also the case for the Compression Indices of the Bangkok Clay. This will be further outlined in the next paragraph.

(iii)   Causes of land subsidence in the Central Plain

The Asian Institute of Technology (AIT, 1985) has defined the main causes of subsidence in the Central Plain as:

1) Overpumping of groundwater through deep well pumping
2) Self weight consolidation of the subsoil
3) Surcharge loading (i.e. buildings, roads and traffic)

a.   Overpumping of groundwater through deep well pumping

The overpumping of groundwater results in a lowering of the pore water pressure in the aquifers and thus the aquitards.

The rate of land subsidence because of the two factors: self-weight loading and surcharge loading depend strongly on the Compression Index. As described in the previous paragraph, this Compression Index is closely related to the type of sediment.

As described earlier, the Bangkok Clay can be subdivided into a stiff clay, a soft clay and a weathered clay. AIT (1981) has tested and summarized the compression indices for these three types of clay.

Table II.5. Overview of general Compression Index Values for clays in the Central Plain
(AIT, 1981)

Type of clay	Compression Index
Soft Clay	0.4 – 1.0
Stiff Clay	-0.1 – -0.2
Deep Clay (that is: clay at greater depth)	0.05 – 0.15

b. *Compression Index of the Soft clay*

The Compression Index is high for the soft Bangkok Clay. There is quite a high variation in the compression Index. This can be explained by differences in facies of the soft Bangkok Clay, as described earlier.

c. *Compression Index of the Stiff clay*

The negative values here for the stiff clay indicate that the clay has been pre-consolidated. There is irrefutable geological evidence that the stiff clay has been buried by other sediments (AIT, 1981). There is geological evidence for this is because the contact between stiff clay and soft clay is an erosional surface. The erosional surface must have been exposed to subaerial erosion for several tens of thousands of years. (AIT, 1981). It is an indication that the stiff clay must have been overlaid with other sediments that were removed later. Another reason why the stiff clay is overconsolidated is explained by desiccation and weathering of the stiff clay (AIT, 1981).

d. *Compression Index of the Deep Clay*

The clays at greater depths have already been loaded by the overlying sediments for a long time span. This means their compression index has been lowered. The compression Index of 0.05-0.15 is indeed relatively low, but still high enough for subsidence to occur. Since there are many clay layers underneath the surface, all with the same C_c-value, together they form quite a large portion of the total land subsidence.

OTHER PROCESSES

e. *Oxidation*

The process of oxidation of peat may also play a role in the total land subsidence, but there is little evidence for presence of peat in the corings. Therefore this process is negligible for the total land subsidence.

f. *Contribution of various layers*

AIT (1981) has investigated the contribution of the consolidation of the Bangkok Clay to the total land subsidence during the first two years: it can be summarized as follows:

Top 50 m-depth range (Bangkok Clay) accounts for 40 per cent of total land subsidence.
Total zone deeper than 50 m accounts for 60 per cent of total land subsidence.

This is in indication that the upper clay layer is quite important to the total land subsidence. However, these results only count for the first two years. The process of consolidation of the upper clay is relatively faster than land subsidence at the lower aquitards. The relative importance of the upper clay layer for the total land subsidence will decrease over the years.

3. Techniques of measuring land subsidence and available data

(i)   General techniques to measure land subsidence

There are two main methods to measure land subsidence:

- Measure the absolute subsidence. This is done by surface leveling, with the use of geodetic techniques.
- Measure the relative subsidence. This is done by measuring the compression of the soil layers. Three types of equipment are used to measure the compression.

Since there exists a relation between subsidence and the pore water pressure in the ground, measuring the pore water pressure is also a way to calculate land subsidence.

a. Absolute Subsidence

Absolute subsidence is the variation in ground elevation against a fixed reference level, such as mean sea level. It requires geodetic survey to measure the changes in elevation. This is the most commonly used source of information about land subsidence in this area.

The equipment designed for measuring the absolute subsidence is called a "surface reference point" or benchmark. The benchmark settles down at the same magnitude as the ground surface. The surface reference point is actually settled one metre in the ground, but the top of the point, a brass ball point, is at the ground surface. The deep stratum benchmark, with its base several metres underground, is not used in this study.

Table II.6. Schematic overview in methods used to measure land subsidence

Quantity	*Method*	*Explanation*
Absolute Subsidence	Surface leveling	Respect to ground surface leveling (benchmark)
		Respect to deep stratum bench mark
	Remote sensing	Radar interferometry
Compression of soil layers	Compression	Shallow type, deep type
	Extension	Cable type, pipe type, bore hole type
	Precision Extensometer	Magnetic, electric resonance, radioactive
Pore water pressure	Aquifer	Piezometer (hydraulic, electric, pneumatic)
		Observation well
	Aquitard	Piezometer (hydraulic, electric, pneumatic)

This method is cheaper than measuring the compression of soil layers with the use of (expensive) compression indicators. Geodetic surveying must be carried out each year.

b. Compression of soil layers

Compression of soil layers: This is carried out at a single point. The total compression is the summation of the compression of the component layers. Three basic types of compression indicators (CI) exist: compression types, extension types and precision extensometers.

(ii) Data sources used in this study

In the area of Bangkok six projects of five organizations or institutes are in use to measure land subsidence. See table II.7 for an overview of the organizations that placed and monitored the equipment.

**Table II.7. Data sources of land subsidence data in the Central Plain
(Data sources marked with an * are used in this study)**

Organization/project	*Bm/station*	*Number*	*Year placed*
AIT (&DMR)*	Both	41	1978, 1982, 1986
MGL-project by DMR*	Both	83	90, 91
RTSD	Benchmark	112	'30, '78, '86, '90, '96
BMA	Benchmarks	116	'79, '86, '90, '96
JICA 1991	Benchmarks	169	1991
JICA 1995	Station	3	1995

Since time was quite limited to do this research, not all these data could be used in this study. The author has limited the data sources to two: the benchmarks installed by AIT/DMR/NEB in 1978 and the benchmarks installed during the MGL-project of the Groundwater Division of DMR.

The reason to choose these two data sources above others was that more detailed information was available, there was a good and reliable description of methods used and the time spans of these two were the longest. Furthermore there were better contacts within these two institutions above the others.

a. AIT Groundwater monitoring stations

In 1978 the Asian Institute of Technology (AIT), together with the Department of Mineral Resources, started a major investigation on the land subsidence in the Bangkok area. During the project several types of equipment (among others: benchmarks) were installed at 27 locations by the Asian Institute of Technology (AIT).

Later, in 1986, the Royal Thai Survey Department (RTSD) installed 14 additional benchmarks. This brings the total number of the benchmarks to 41.

Table II.8. Number and dates of surveys of AIT stations
(Note time gap between surveys no. 7 and 8)

No.	Dates of surveys Start	Finish	Existing datapoints	Leveled datapoints	% of total leveled
1	May-78	Sept.-78	27		
2	Oct.-78	Jan.-79	27	16	
3	Feb.-79	May-79	27	19	
4	Aug.-79	Nov.-79	27	21	
5	Feb.-80	May-80	27	21	
6	Aug.-80	Nov.-80	27	21	
7	Mar.-81	Jun.-81	27	21	
8	Nov.-84	Apr.-85	27	21	
9	Nov.-85	Apr.-86	27	21	
10	Nov.-86	Apr.-87	41	21	
11	Feb.-88	Aug.-88	41	22	
12	Nov.-88	May-89	41	22	
13	Nov.-89	Apr.-90	41	22	
14	Nov.-90	Apr.-91	41	22	
15	Nov.-91	May-92	41	22	
16	Dec.-92	Jun.-93	41	22	
17	Apr.-94	Sept.-94	41	17	
18	Jan.-95	Jun.-95	41	15	
19	Jan.-96	Jun.-96	41	15	
20	Dec.-96	July-97	41	15	
21	Nov.-97	Jan.-98	41	12	
22	Jan.-99	Sept.-99	41	8	
23	Dec.-99	May-00	41	7	

b. MGL-project

In 1985 a new project was initiated by the DMR: "The Mitigation of Groundwater crisis and Land-subsidence in the Bangkok Area" (MGL). A total number of 103 groundwater-monitoring stations were placed, measuring the height of the piezometric level in three aquifers: Phra Pradaeng, Nakhon Luang and Nontha Buri. Later on, in 1990 and 1991 a total of 83 new 1-m depth benchmarks were installed. These benchmarks were installed all over the Central Plain, covering an area of 6,400 km^2. See figure II.8 for the location of these benchmarks.

The DMR's Groundwater Survey Division has carried out land surface leveling of these benchmarks every year. Distraction of the topographic height over two years gives the subsidence in that particular year. The first survey was carried out in 1991; this gives the topographic height of those points. Thus in the second year, 1992, the first rate of subsidence could be calculated.

Unfortunately, not all the data of the surface levelings of these benchmarks is available to the author. An overview of the data availability is given in table II.9.

Table II.9. Surveys carried out over the MGL-project datapoints, and the number and percentage leveled in the respective studies

Year	Existing datapoints	Leveled datapoints	% of total that is leveled
1991	83	35	42%
1992	83	75	90%
1993	83	81	98%
1994	83	83	100%
1995	83	83	100%
1996	83	83	100%
1997	83	41	49%
1998	83	4	5%
1999	83	58	70%
2000	83	57	69%

4. Maps showing land subsidence in the Bangkok area

(i) Methodology to create the maps

To create the maps showing land subsidence the SURFER software was used. The spreadsheet data were imported into this programme.

To create the contour maps the kriging method was used. This widely used, geostatistical gridding method produces visually appealing maps from irregularly spaced data. Kriging attempts to express trends suggested in the data, so that, for example, high points might be connected along a ridge rather than by so-called isolated bull's eye contours.

It must be noted, however, that the kriging geostatistical method of the SURFER software not always gives a 'common sense' result. This is a big disadvantage of computerized contouring over a more or less 'subjective' contouring, with the knowledge of geology and locations of groundwater pumping in mind. Thus, some contourlines of equal land subsidence, especially near the edges of the produced maps, may not represent the actual land subsidence.

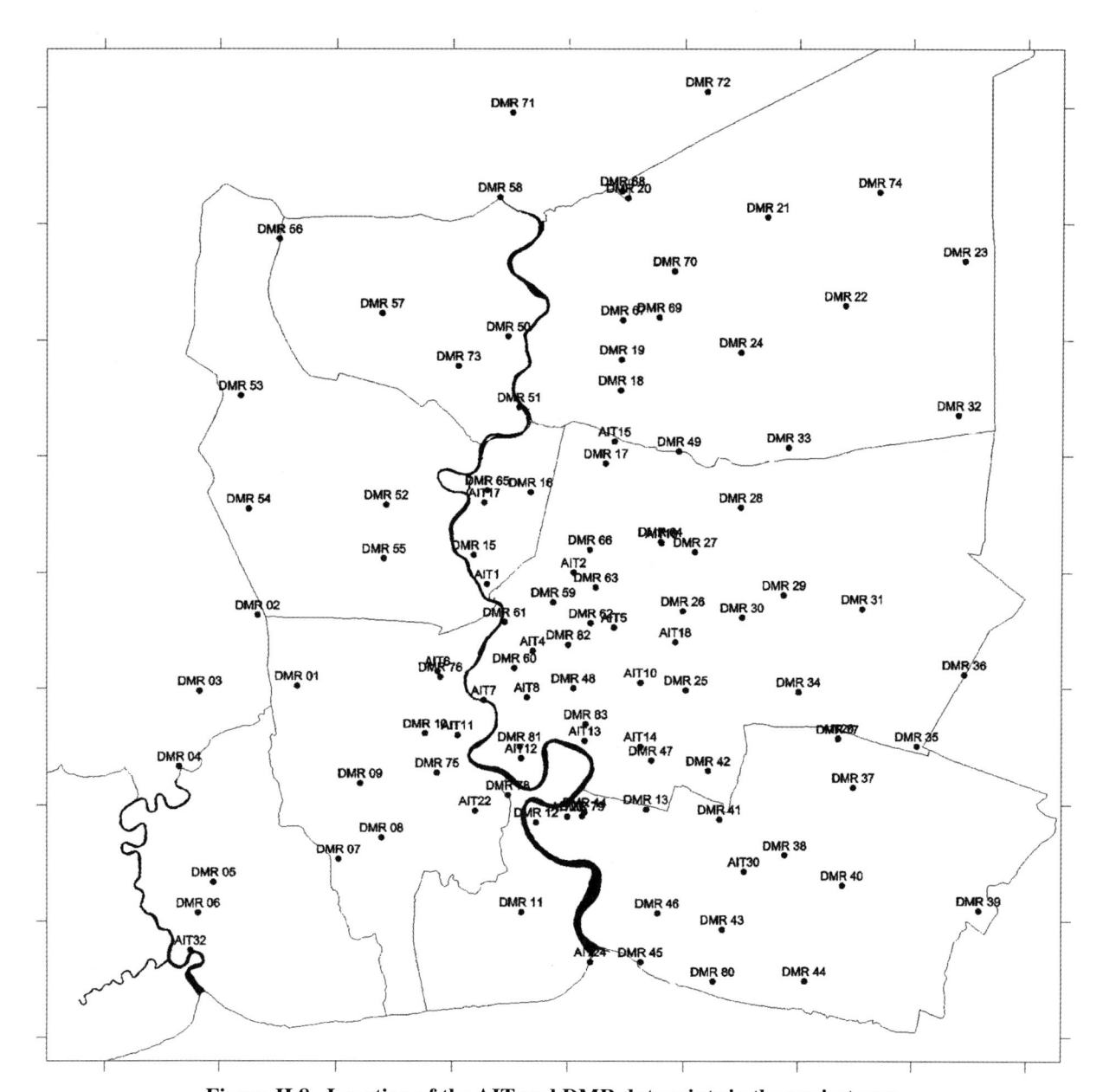

Figure II.8. Location of the AIT and DMR datapoints in the project area

(ii)   Land subsidence maps: single years

Land subsidence can be mapped for every year for which (sufficient) data are available. In the following some maps will be described and discussed.

Figure II.9 shows the land subsidence in 2000. Land subsidence is at its maximum near Lat Krabang, 4.75 m in the last year. Also the area near Samut Sakhon shows quite high values: more than 3 cm land subsidence in the last year.

The year 1979 was the year with the maximum land subsidence in the Bangkok Area: more than 12 cm per year! The centre of the subsidence bowl is near Bang Kapi.

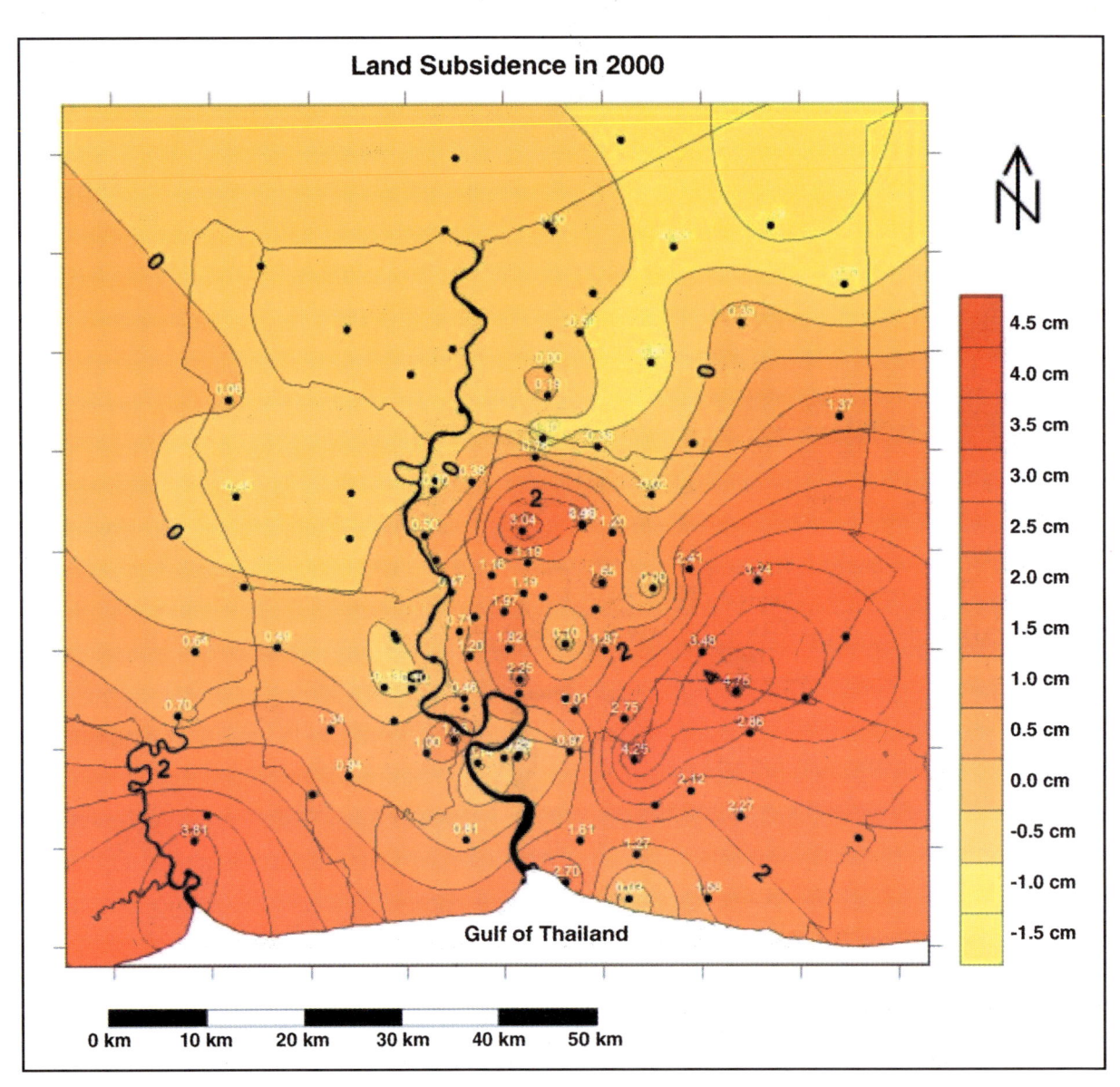

Figure II.9. Land subsidence in the year 2000

Atlas of Urban Geology – Volume 13

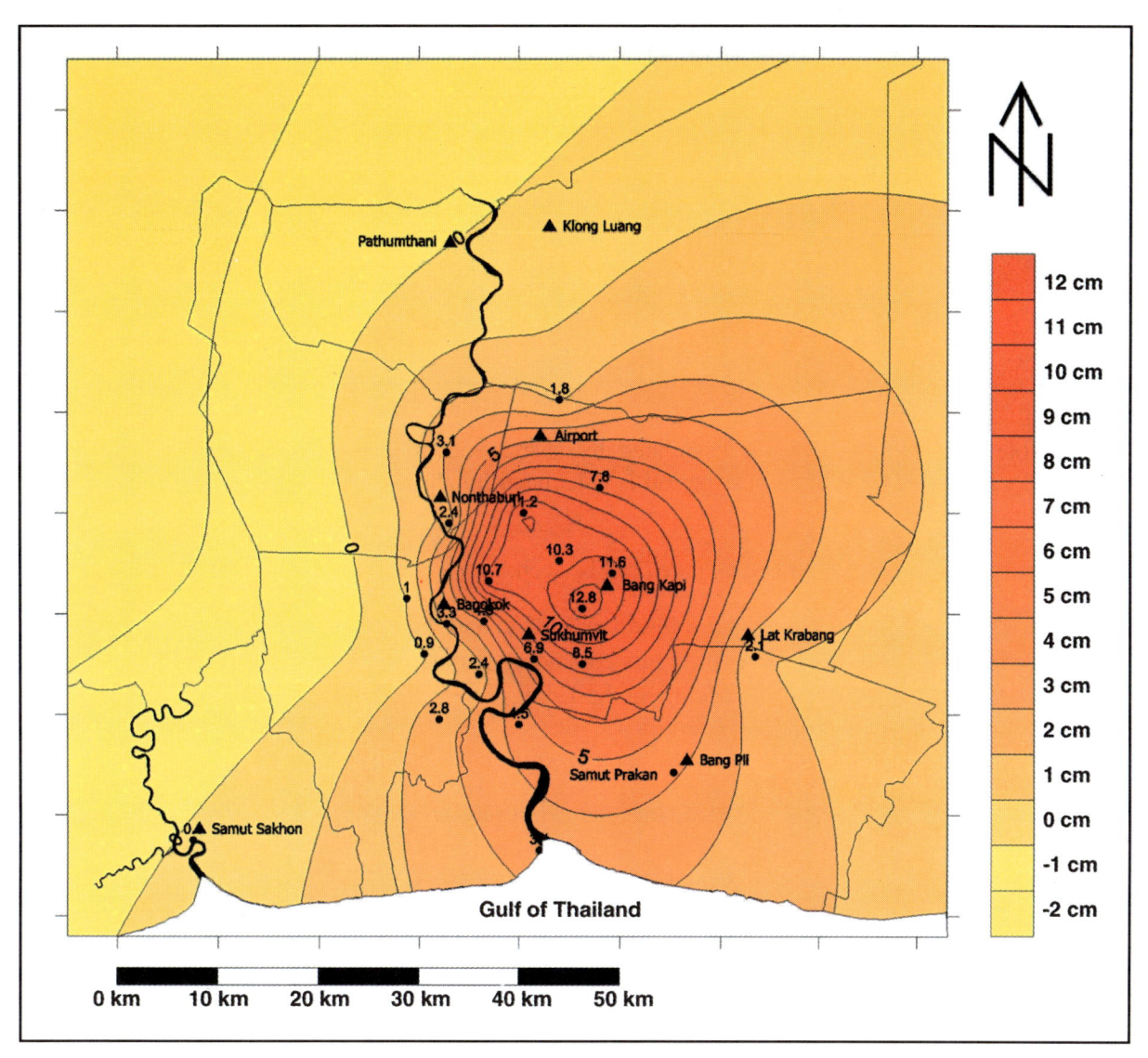

Figure II.10. Land subsidence in the year 1979

(iii)   Land subsidence maps: three-year periods

The timespan between the first survey (1978) and the last (2000) is rather large. It is too large to get a good overview of the changes in rate and magnitude of land subsidence over the years. To overcome this problem, the time span of 22 years is divided into seven periods of three years each; (the second period is four years).

Table II.10. Overview of periods used to show land subsidence

Period number	Years
Period 1	1978 – '79 – '80 – '81
Period 2	1981 – '82 – '83 – '84 – '85
Period 3	1985 – '86 – '87 – '88
Period 4	1988 – '89 – '90 – '91
Period 5	1991 – '92 – '93 – '94
Period 6	1994 – '95 – '96 – '97
Period 7	1997 – '98 – '99 – 2000

Note: Land subsidence is calculated by abstraction of the elevation between two years. Thus land subsidence for a three-year period is calculated by abstracting the elevation in year x from the elevation in year x+3.

From the maps three explicit changes can be seen:

1. The effect of the cabinet's resolution of 1983 to halt the groundwater pumping
2. Expansion of the city over the years coinciding with land subsidence
3. Economic prosperity and decline in the 1990s

a.   The effect of the cabinet resolution on groundwater pumping

When we compare the rate of land subsidence in the second and third period, we see that the land subsidence in the second period is very high, but that the rate of subsidence is very low in the third period. This is due to the implemented resolution of the Cabinet that halted the groundwater pumping. From 1983 onwards MWA started phasing out its groundwater pumpage.

b.   Expansion of the city over the years and coinciding land subsidence

The city expanded over the years and the centre of the subsidence bowl shifted with it. In 1978 the centre was south-west of Bang Kapi. In the period 1997-2000 the centre of the subsidence bowl was near Lat Krabang.

c.   Economic prosperity and decline in the 1990s

When we compare the two maps of the periods 1994-1997 and 1997-2000, we can see that the rate of land subsidence in the first period is much higher than in the second period. This can be explained by the economic prosperity in Thailand in that period, when Bangkok experienced an economic boom. After the economic downturn, groundwater demand lowered. The rate of subsidence lowered as a direct consequence.

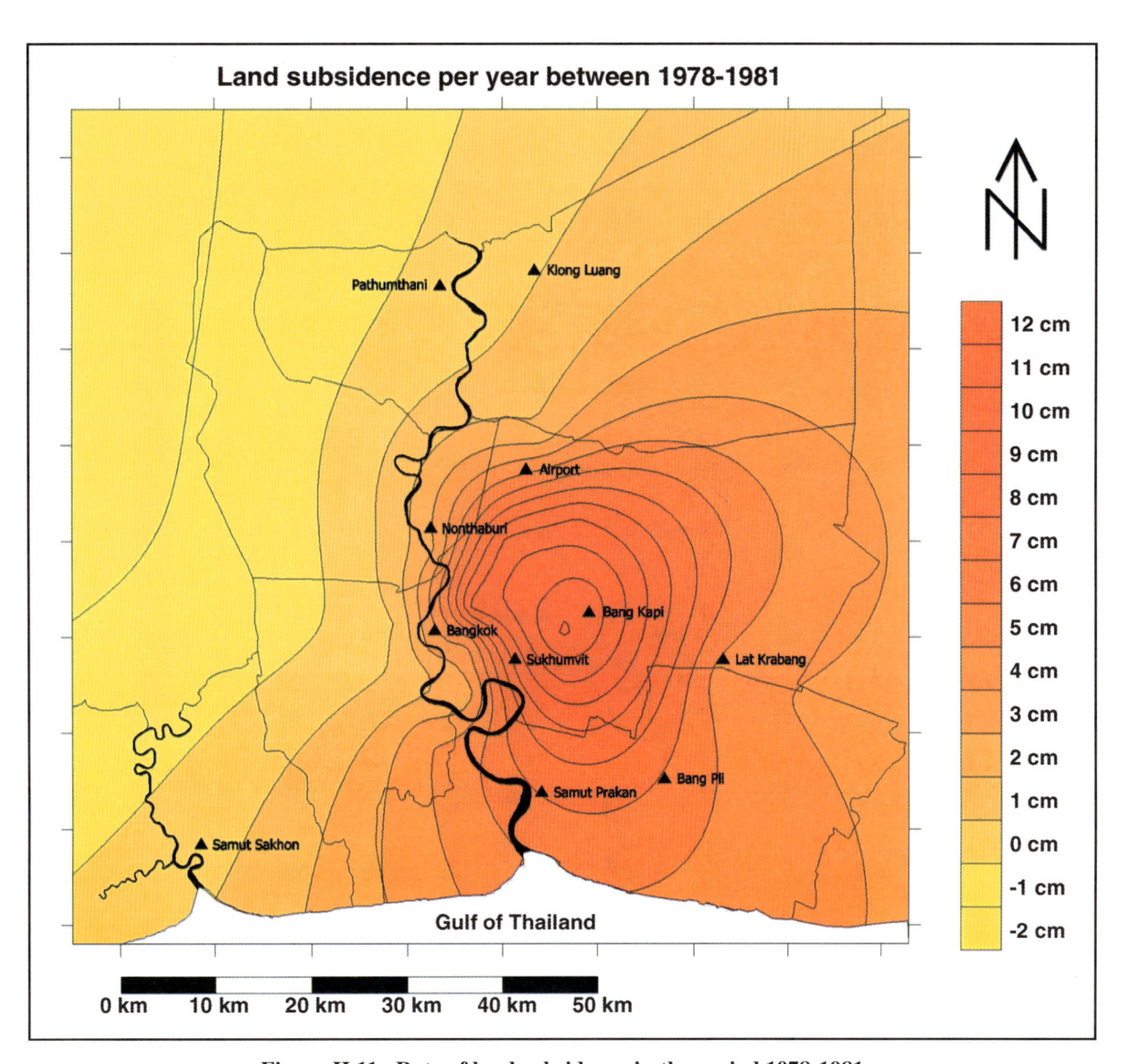

Figure II.11. Rate of land subsidence in the period 1978-1981

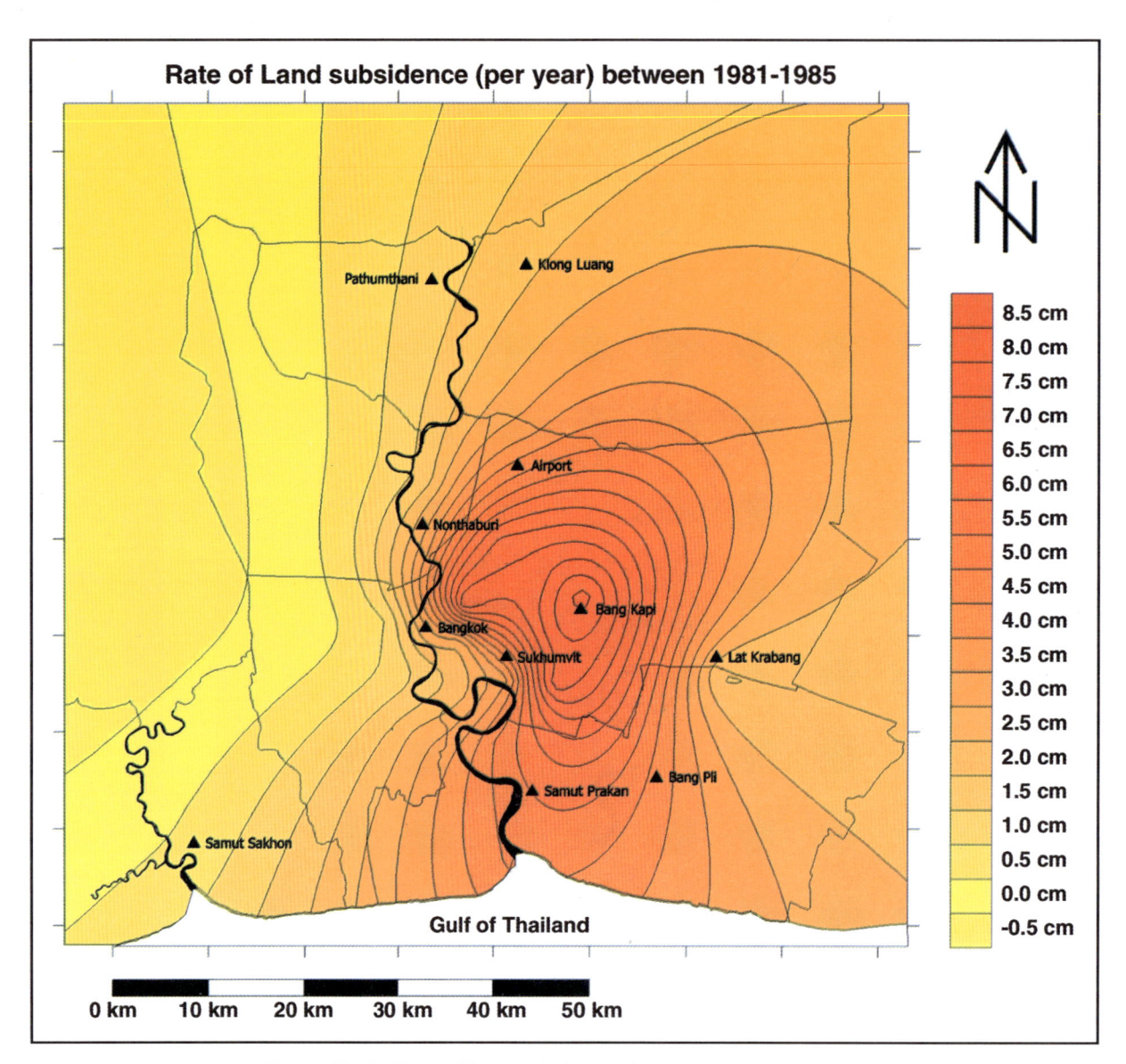

Figure II.12. Rate of land subsidence in the period 1981-1985

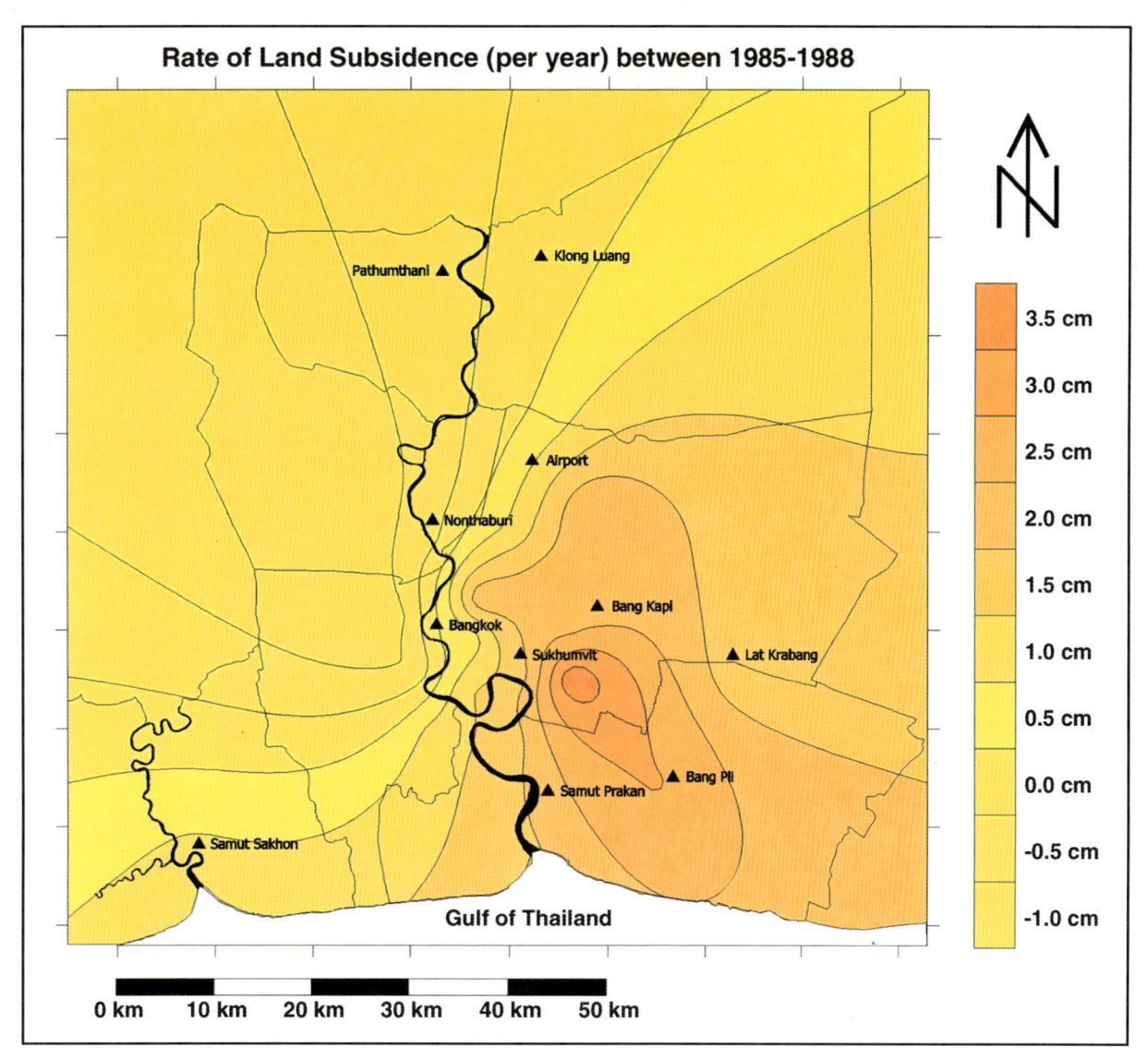

Figure II.13. Rate of land subsidence in the period 1985-1988

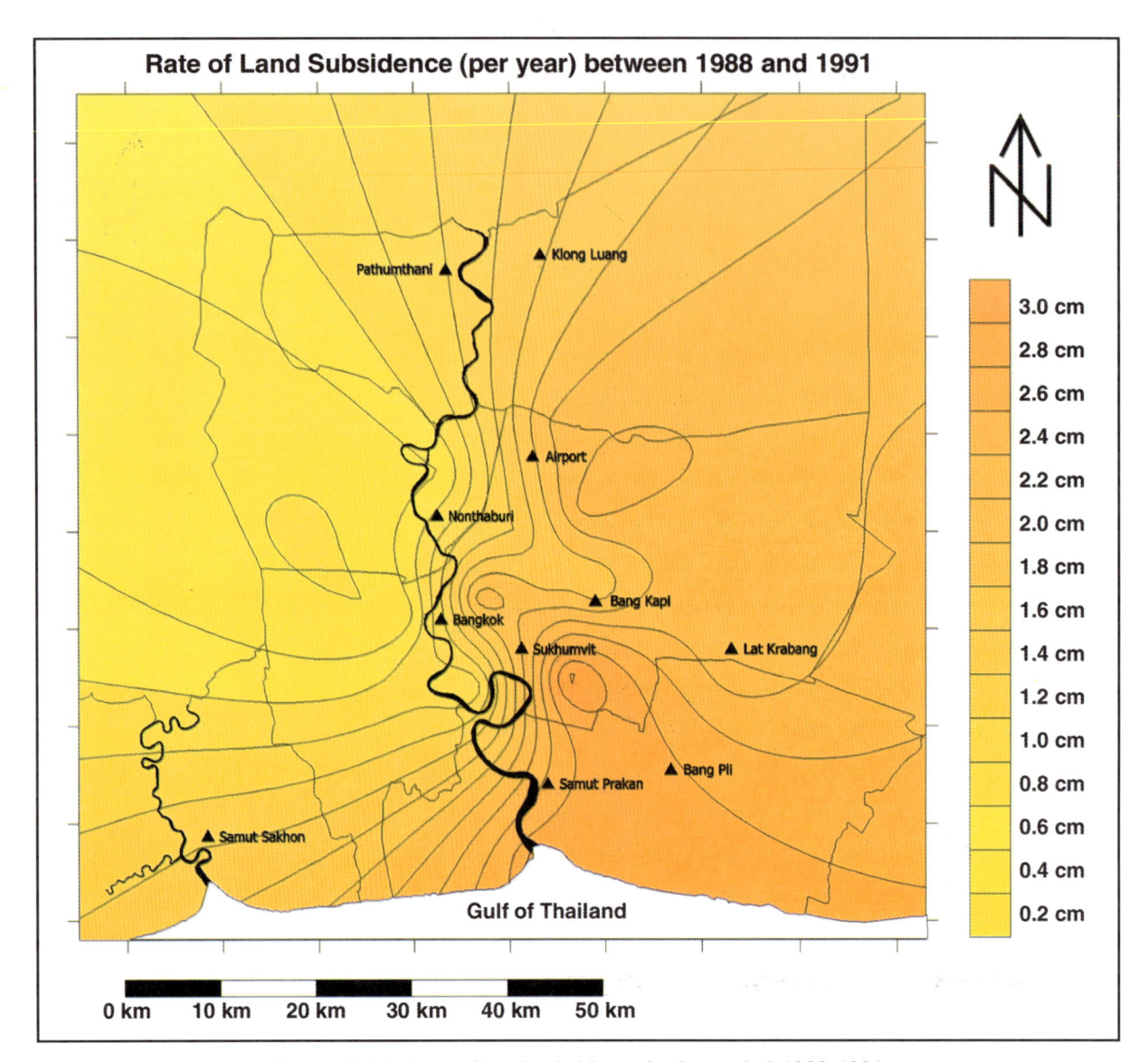

Figure II.14. Rate of land subsidence in the period 1988-1991

Atlas of Urban Geology – Volume 13

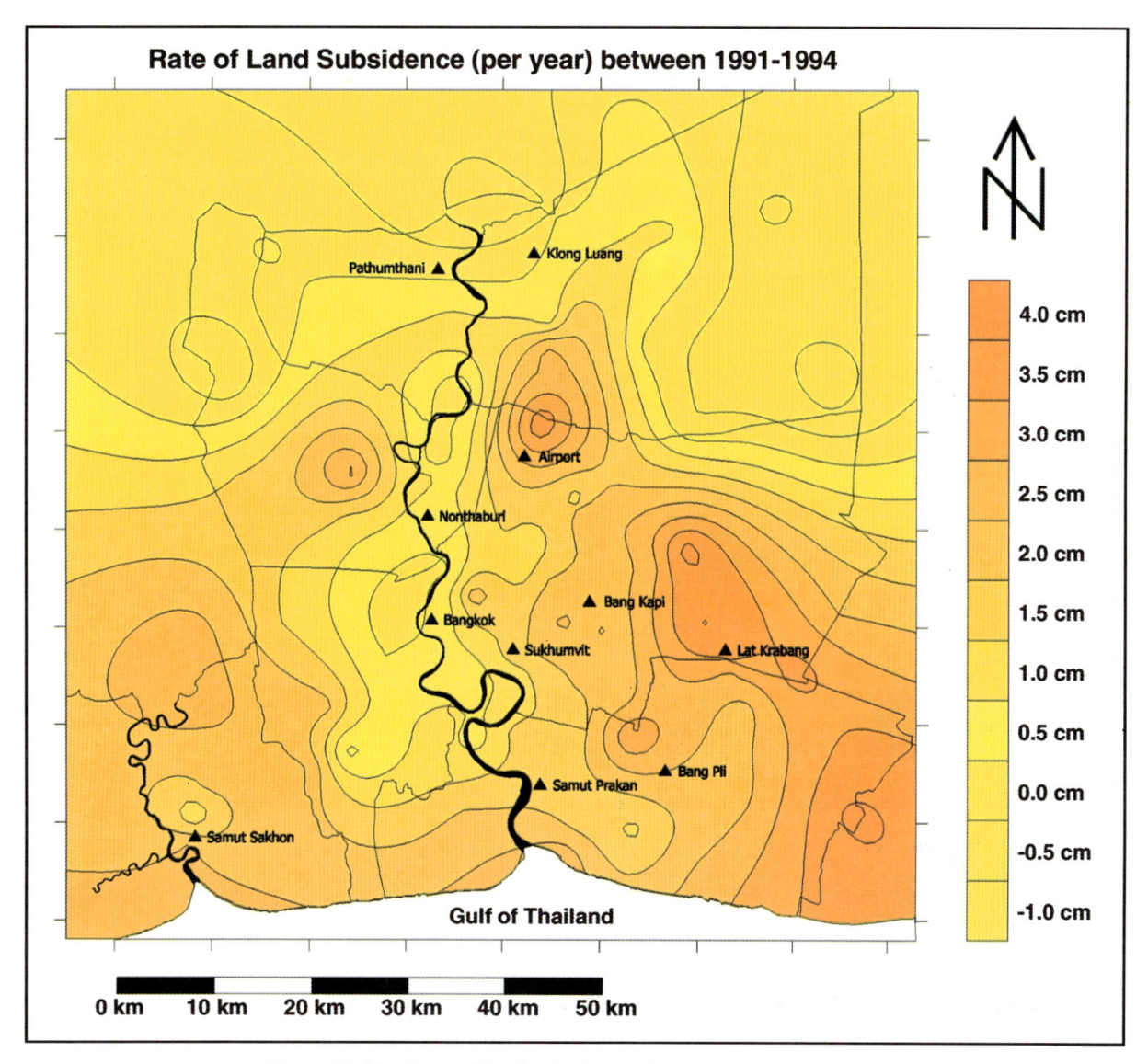

Figure II.15. Rate of land subsidence in the period 1991-1994

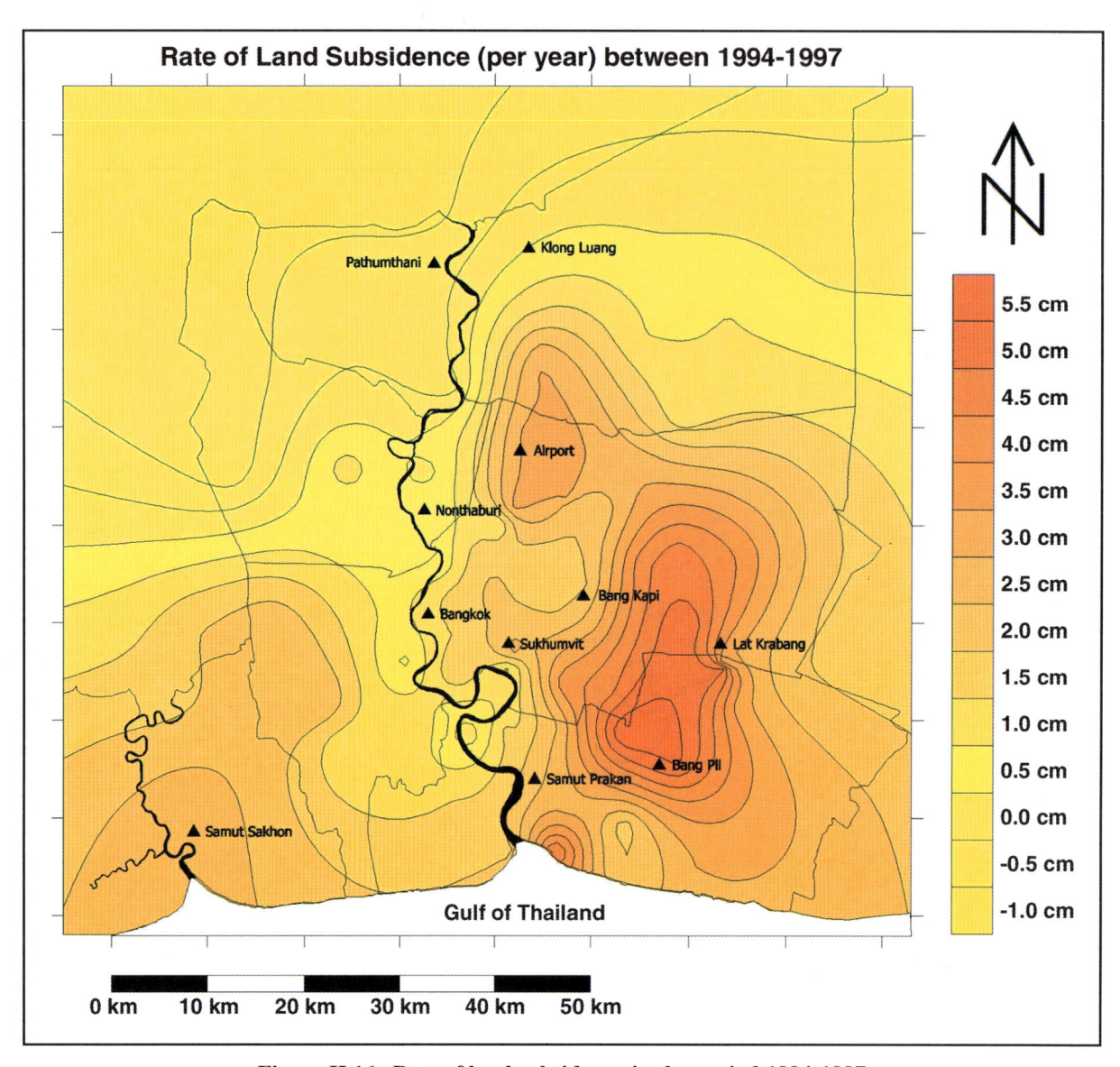

Figure II.16. Rate of land subsidence in the period 1994-1997

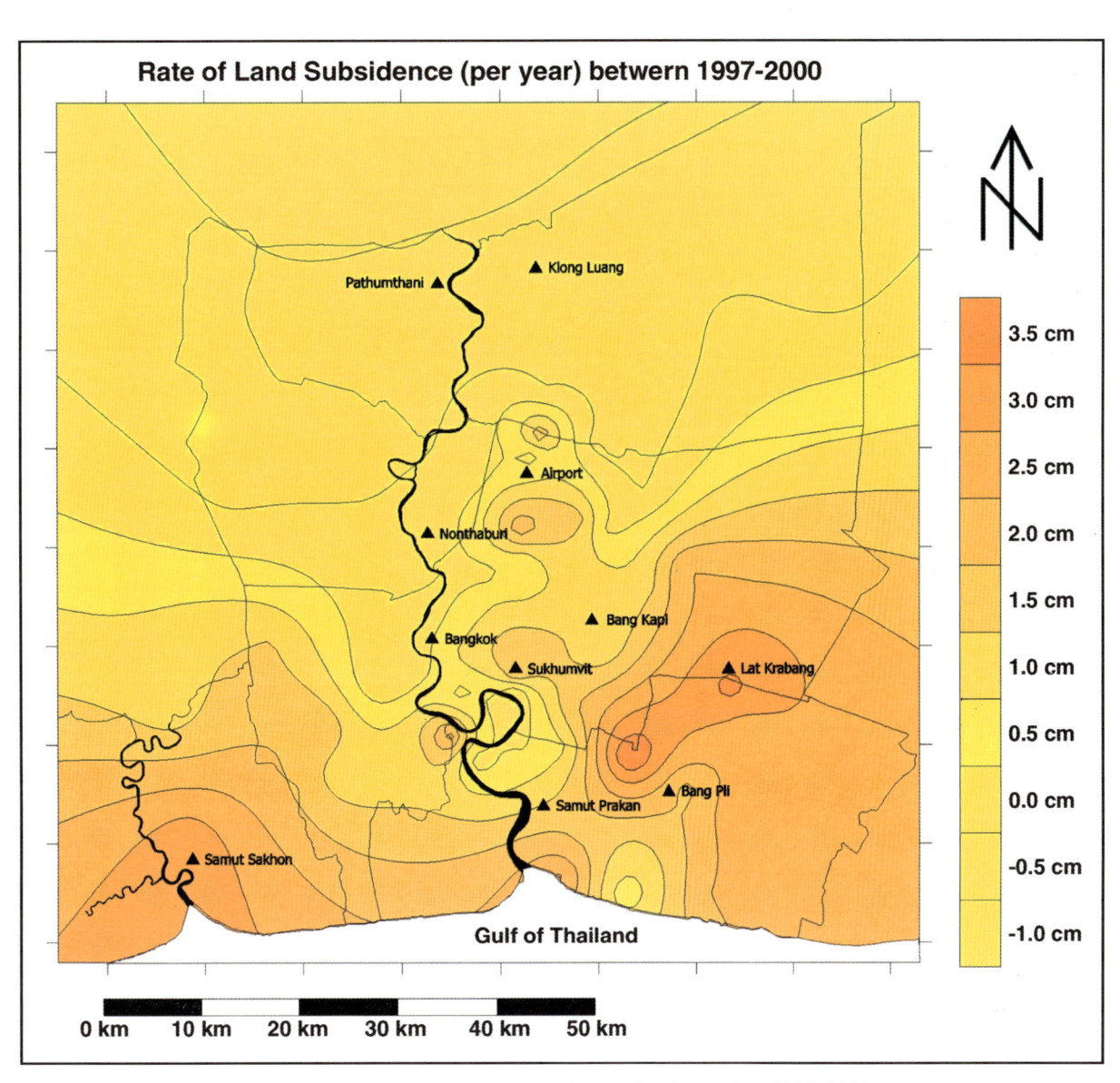

Figure II.17. Rate of land subsidence in the period 1997-2000

(iv)   Land subsidence maps: whole period

I have created two maps: one map that shows the total land subsidence since 1978, this map is based on data from the AIT monitoring stations. The other map shows the total land subsidence between 1992 and 2000, this map is based on both data sets.

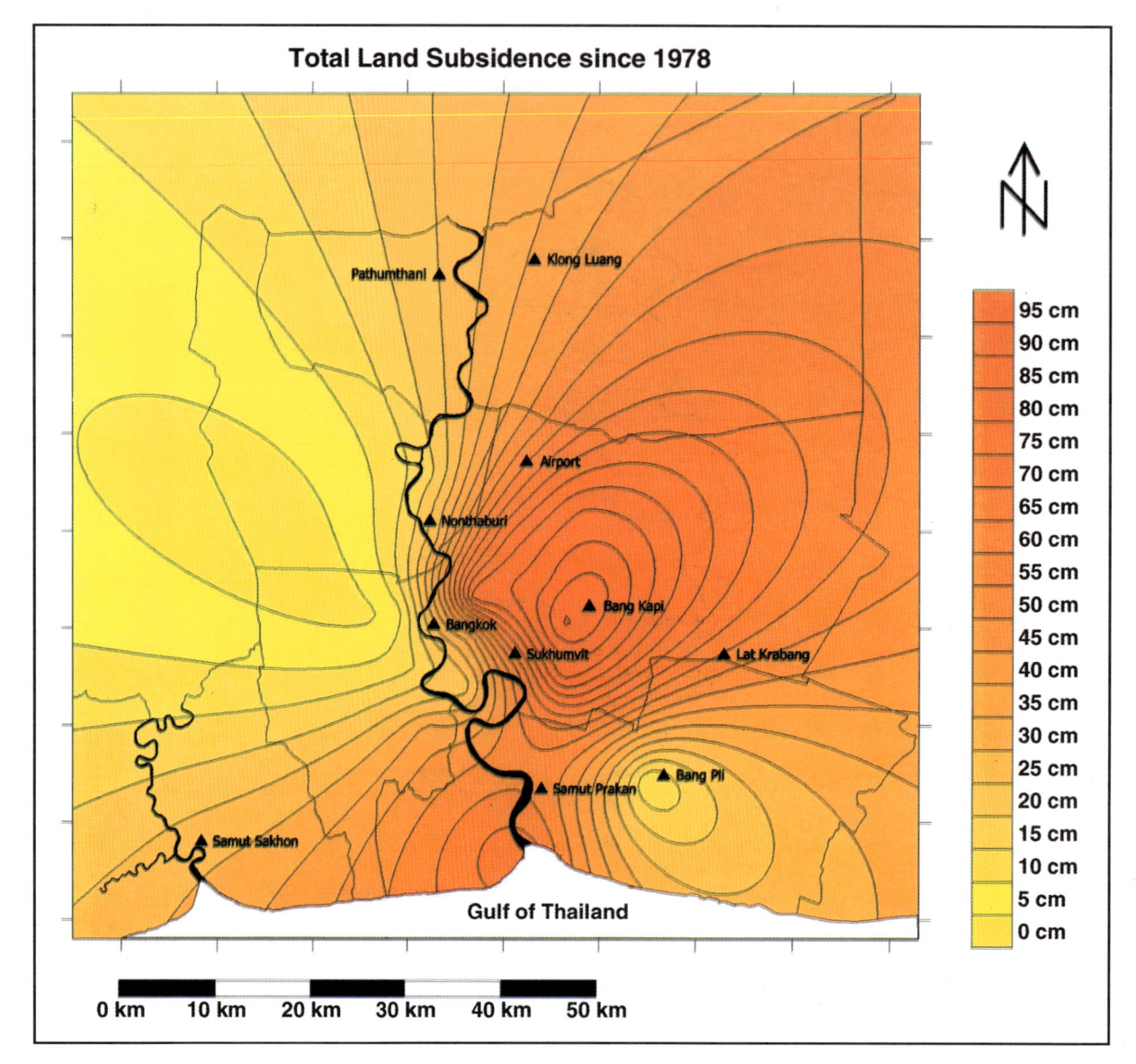

Figure II.18. Total land subsidence between 1978 and 2000
(based on the AIT database)

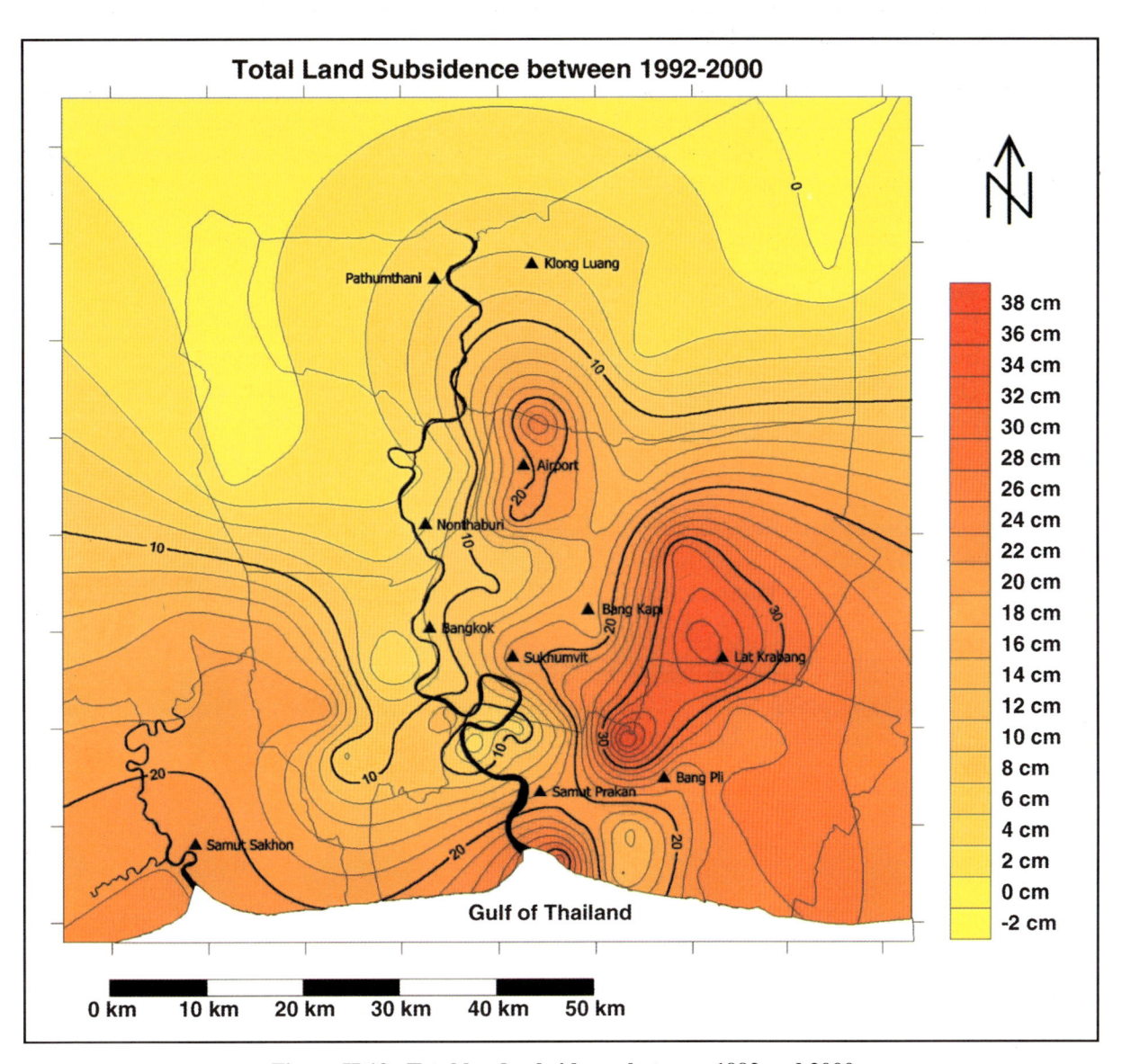

Figure II.19. Total land subsidence between 1992 and 2000

D. Consequences of land subsidence and the overpumping of groundwater

1. Introduction

In this chapter the consequences of land subsidence and the overpumping of groundwater in the Bangkok area are discussed and described.

It is noteworthy that the visible and concrete consequences are quite well understood by various researchers. However, since these effects are occurring in a rather large area, it is impossible to produce an estimation of the total cost of the problem of land subsidence. Furthermore, it is beyond the scope of this report to give such a prediction.

Three categories of physical consequences of land subsidence can be distinguished:

1. Prolonged and extended flooding by river- and/or seawater.
2. Damage to the infrastructure such as to the foundations of buildings, roads, bridges and buried pipelines. Also water well head protrusion above the surface occurs.
3. Disturbance and deterioration of the drainage system (canals and wastewater sewers) because of the development of subsidence bowls.

These three categories are further outlined in paragraphs 2, 3 and 4, respectively.

The large amount of groundwater that is pumped out of the Bangkok soils (overpumping) results in the intrusion of saline water in the upper aquifers. As a result, some wells in those aquifers have been abandoned. The consequences of intrusion of saline water are further described in paragraph 5.

Not only related to land subsidence but nevertheless a major problem for the area, is the coastal erosion that takes places at the coast of the Upper Gulf of Thailand in which the Bangkok area is situated. Some remarks on this coastal erosion are presented in paragraph 6.

2. Prolonged and extended flooding

(i)   General

Floodings in Thailand are caused by high precipitation in a short time interval and increased runoff. Land subsidence does not cause the floodings, but it will prolong the time an area is flooded and the area that is affected by floodings, will be larger.

Especially in 1983 there was a major flooding and large areas of Bangkok were flooded for about three months. The ESCAP secretariat (1990) has studied the causes of the severe floodings of 1983 and they can be summarized as follows:

- Local heavy rainfall (575 mm in August en 454 mm in September).
- High flows in the Chao Phraya River from the north.
- The back-up effect of high tides on the Chao Phraya River.
- In-land sheet flow from the north and east.
- Continuing land subsidence.
- Insufficient drainage capacity.
- A change in land-use conditions, resulting in a decrease in the water-retaining capacity (that is: more concrete surfaces instead of arable land).

a. Flooding and agriculture

A number of important physical and chemical processes occur when arable land is flooded. (Source: humid tropical environments)

- The breakdown of aggregates in the soil.
- An almost complete denitrification of nitrate occurs.
- Large, and sometimes toxic, amounts of CO_2 are released from the soil. The CO_2 will be toxic to the roots of plants.
- Reduction processes will occur, changing the chemical processes in the soil.
- When salt water inundates the floodplain the soil will become too acid, due to chemical processes. (This happens in so-called *acid sulfate soils or cat clay* of which there are many in the Central Plain).

All these processes can take place and as a consequence they will harm agricultural production in the area that is flooded by the rivers.

(ii) Flooding and health

When areas are flooded, the water can bring many types of water-borne diseases. For example, cholera, typhoid, dysentery, gastroenteritis, infectious hepatitis and diarrhea can occur. This is because during such flooding the mixing of garbage, excrements and water occurs, which has proved in the past to be a major recipe for health catastrophes. Furthermore, flooded areas form an excellent breeding ground for mosquitoes. They can spread, among others, *Urban filariasis*; a blood parasite that is very common in Southeast Asia and especially prevalent where unsanitary conditions exist in urban areas (ESCAP secretariat, 1990, after Camp, Dresser and McKee, 1970).

It is to note that flooding has always occurred in the low Central Plain of Thailand but nowadays the combination of a high population density in the Bangkok area and flooding can now easily cause an outbreak of water-borne diseases.

Another aspect of flooding that has been observed is that many persons have died because of electrocution due to short-circuiting.

(iii) Tidal floods

During spring tide, a tidal event that happens every two weeks, the water level in some smaller coastal areas is so high that roads and other land will be inundated. The land subsidence has increased the magnitude and extension of this specific type of flooding.

Figure II.20. Tidal flood in Phra Pradaeng, near the Chao Phraya River mouth
(Photo courtesy of NEDECO)

3. Damage to the infrastructure

(i)   Breakage of sewers and pipelines

Some studies estimate that in general about 40-50 per cent of all sewage and water pipes in the Bangkok area, especially the older parts of the city, is broken. Land subsidence is a major cause of the breakage of these pipes, but it is not the only cause. Other causes are bad construction, bad or no maintenance and chemical decomposition of the water lines due to the acid soils in this region. (ESCAP secretariat, 1988). The following case study reveals some aspects of this problem.

a.   Case study: the Huay Kwang Waste Water Treatment Plant

This Waste Water Treatment Plant (WWTP) was built in 1975 in a northern part of Bangkok. In this area the land subsidence is and was quite high and a total subsidence of about 80 cm was measured at the AIT benchmarks in the direct vicinity since 1978.

The WWTP was designed to treat the amount of 2,400 m^3 wastewater per day that is generated by the about 16,800 persons living in the area it covers. Due to breakage of many wastewater sewers leading to the WWTP, the maximum inflow to the WWTP is only 1,100 m^3/day at present. It has even been lower at a rate of some 900 m^3/day before the renovation of the sewers was carried out in 1995. Hence, the WWTP functions only at half capacity at the moment and the remaining wastewater (2,400 m^3/day − 1,100 m^3/day = 1,300 m^3/day) leaks into the ground. This will pollute the groundwater and increase the risk for a number of water-borne diseases as described in paragraph 2. *(ii)* above.

Atlas of Urban Geology – Volume 13 71

Figure II.21. Land subsidence at the Huay Kwai Waste Water Treatment Plant.
The surface was originally connected to the building. Since the building is on piles
resting on the bearing sand layer, and the road is not, the latter subsided

Figure II.22. Land subsidence at the Huay Kwai WWTP. The end of the drainpipe must have been
only slightly above the ground surface. Its end is now about 70 cm above the ground.
The arrow indicates the former ground level.

(ii)   Damage to roads and bridges

The land subsidence causes problems to roads and bridges. The consolidation of the Bangkok clay, both caused by natural settlement and by distraction of the groundwater, causes the lowering of the ground surface and hence the roads on top of it. Since the bridges are built with their foundations on the bearing sand layer (approximately 20 m deep) and the roads themselves are not founded, this may lead to a break of the interfaces between the road and bridge. For an example of this see figure II.23.

Figure II.23. Damage to a bridge in the old town of Bangkok (Charoen Krung Road); extra steps are necessary for pedestrians to enter the bridge

Figure II.24. Damage to a pavement in Bang Kapi. Note the differences in height between the unfounded road and the founded building.

Also, the differences in soil settlement and land subsidence will deteriorate the quality of the road. This means for the Bangkok area that roads have to be maintained almost every year. The total cost of this maintenance has been estimated at about two billion baht (US $45 million) per year (Singapore Straits Times Interactive, August 2000).

(iii) Well head protrusion

Water well heads can protrude when land subsidence occurs. This is due to the fact that the bottom of such a well is fixed to a sand layer. When the uppermost sediments are compressed and compacted, the well head will finally protrude above the surface. This will cause problems with water pumping.

4. Deterioration of the natural drainage system

Flood barriers that have to protect most areas of Bangkok were designed in the year 1995. The maximum height reserved by the construction team for land subsidence of the barriers to occur is about 0.40 m (NEDECO, 1996).

Some problems with the flow of water through the canals (*klongs*) will arise with newly formed bowls due to land subsidence. These subsidence bowls will stagnate the flow of water through the *klongs* and some flood-prone areas will be developed in the centre of the subsidence bowl. See figure II.25 for a map of the location of the two main subsidence bowls.

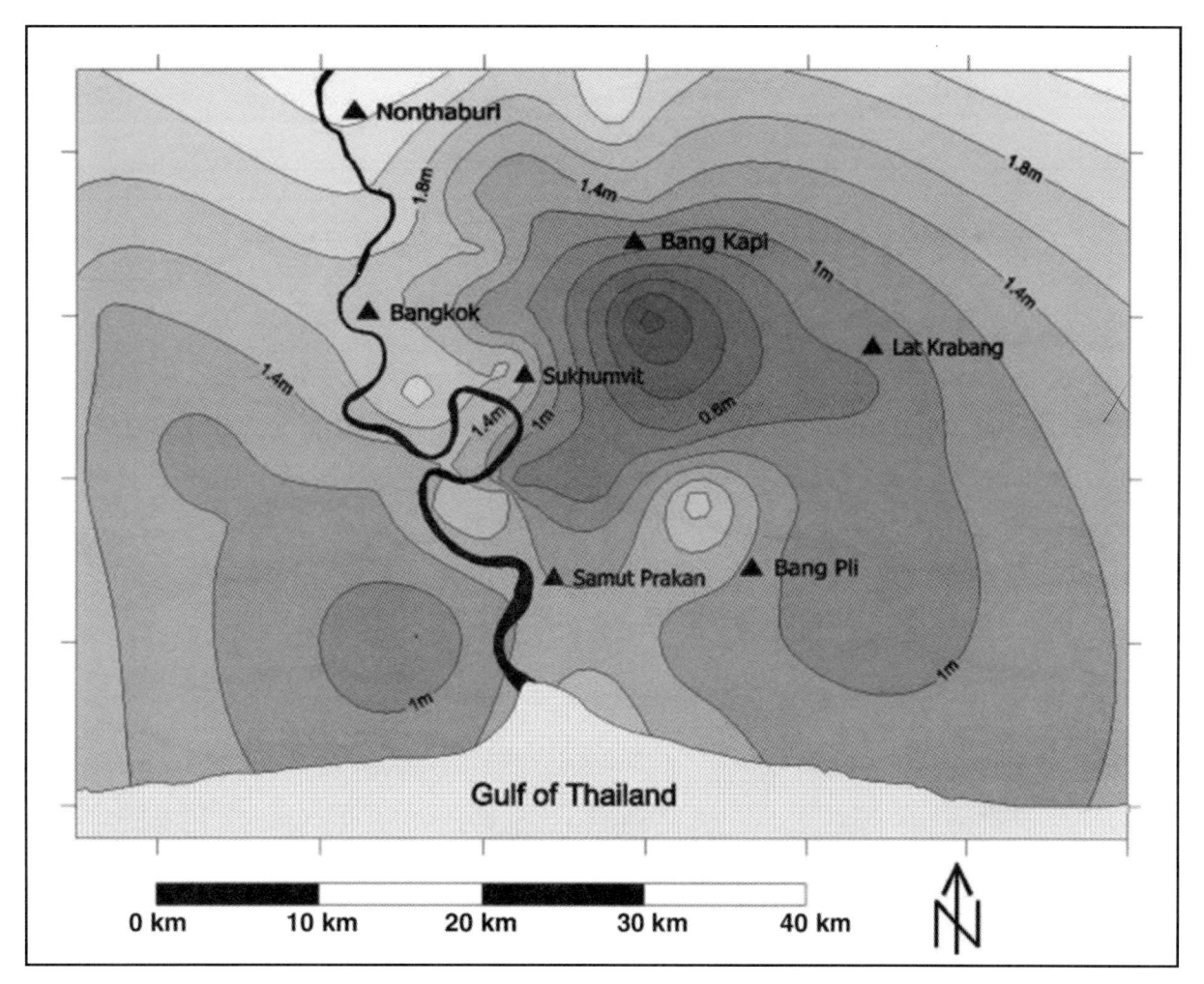

Figure II.25. A land subsidence bowl has developed in Eastern Bangkok. The deepest point of the bowl is just below 0 m and is therefore more than 1 metre lower than the surrounding area.

5. Intrusion of saline water

(i)   General

A consequence of the lowering of the piezometric level of the aquifers is the intrusion of seawater in the aquifers. Intrusion of saline water was first discovered in 1967 when municipal wells in the western and southern part of Bangkok yielded brackish to saline water.

In their natural state, the aquifers of the Bangkok Multi Aquifer system contain a distribution of both fresh and saline groundwater. Because of the different densities of fresh and saline water the system tends to a hydrostatic equilibrium, with a wedge of saline water in the aquifer. When the piezometric level in the aquifer is lowered, the hydrostatic equilibrium is out of balance and protrusion of saline water in the aquifer takes place (UNESCO, 1998). See figure II.26 for a graphical explanation of the situation.

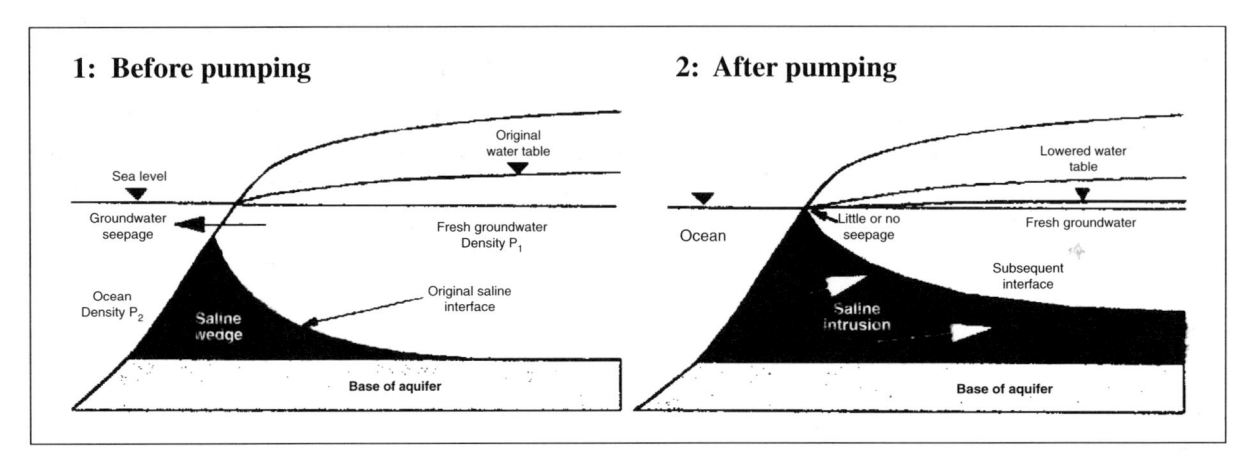

Figure II.26. Principle of saline groundwater intrusion in an aquifer
(UNESCO 1998, after Siegel, 1996)

Obviously, the rate of saltwater intrusion is higher where the groundwater level is lower due to over-pumping of the aquifers.

It was observed that not only the chloride content was higher after the intrusion, but increases in water hardness and iron, manganese, sulfate, calcium, sodium, magnesium and dissolved solids also occurred (Ramnarong and Buapeng, 1992).

The consequences of salt water intrusion are:

- Groundwater becomes undrinkable and wells will have to be abandoned.
- Intruded saline water harms the agricultural production.
- Environmental and vegetational changes.

(ii)   Dispersion

A well-known problem in the soil sciences is the problem of dispersion. Dispersive soils contain a certain clay fraction that has a high potential to be in a dispersive state when the soil mass will come in contact with saline water. This problem especially occurs after reclamation of mangrove forests for agricultural (or aquacultural) purposes. As a result the clay becomes too acid for agriculture.

This problem may also affect the deep clays of the Bangkok clay layers. Some geochemical processes might occur, causing the clay aggregates to break up. The newly formed clay particles may dissolve in the groundwater. This will lead to larger voids. This in turn, as described in paragraph 2, can lead to enhanced land subsidence. Unfortunately, little evidence for this is available and more fundamental research is needed on this subject.

6. Coastal erosion

In the provinces of Samut Prakan, Bangkok and Samut Sakhon on the coast of the Upper Gulf of Thailand, significant coastal erosion takes place. The rate has been assessed as approximately 5 metres per year.

There are several reasons for this coastal erosion:

- Less sediment in the Chao Phraya River because of dredging upstream.
- Destruction of the mangrove coast due to human activities.
- Changes in circulation pattern in the Gulf of Thailand, causing erosion.
- Land subsidence causing a relative sea level rise.

(i)   Land subsidence compared with sea level rise

When we compare the total land subsidence in the Samut Prakan area over the last 22 years with the total eustatic sea-level rise, it is clear that the amount of land subsidence is larger than the eustatic sea-level rise. The land subsidence for Samut Prakan area is approximately 40 mm per year as shown in figure II.27. The eustatic sea level rose about 1.5-2 mm per year during the twentieth century as is measured by tide gauges worldwide. (IPCC, 2001). Consequently, the rate of land subsidence measured at the coast of Samut Prakan is more than twenty times higher than the rate of eustatic sea-level rise.

New predictions made by the Intergovernmental Panel on Climate Change (IPCC) in the spring of 2001 show an estimated eustatic sea-level rise of 0.45 m for the 21st century (medium scenario). The maximum estimated sea-level rise for the next hundred years is 0.88 m (high scenario) and the minimum is 0.09 m (low scenario). This means that also in the future the land subsidence in this area will be probably significantly higher than the predicted eustatic sea-level rise.

(ii)   Coastal erosion

Coastal erosion is occurring between the mouths of the Ta Chin and Chao Phraya Rivers. It is difficult to estimate, but the coastline may have receded about 300-400 m in the last decades. No exact rate is known at present. Vongvissomjai (1990) calculated the coastal erosion and accretion around the Chao Phraya River mouth. Between 1969 and 1987 the total coastal erosion, occurring at the West Side of the mouth, was estimated as 7.2×10^6 m^2. However no estimations of recedence of the coastline are known. On the East Side the total accretion in this period was about 3.4×10^6 m^2 (Jaruponsakul, 1999 after Vongvissomjai, 1990). These local processes of erosion and accretion might be caused by processes in the Chao Phraya River and does not necessarily have the same rate at other locations along the coast (Westerwerp, pers. comm).

One main cause of coastal erosion is the reduced amount of sediment in the Chao Phraya River. Due to the constructions of dams the total amount of silt in the river has receded with about 80 per cent (NEDECO, 1987). Also upstream sand-dredging activities (for the cement industries of Bangkok) have had their influence on the sediment transport in the river. Also the Bangkok Port is a major sink for silt, each year dredging is necessary to maintain the depth of the harbor. This decrease in sediment load has, of course, a big influence on the position and morphology of the coastline.

Subsidence at the Samut Prakan Coast (AIT 24)

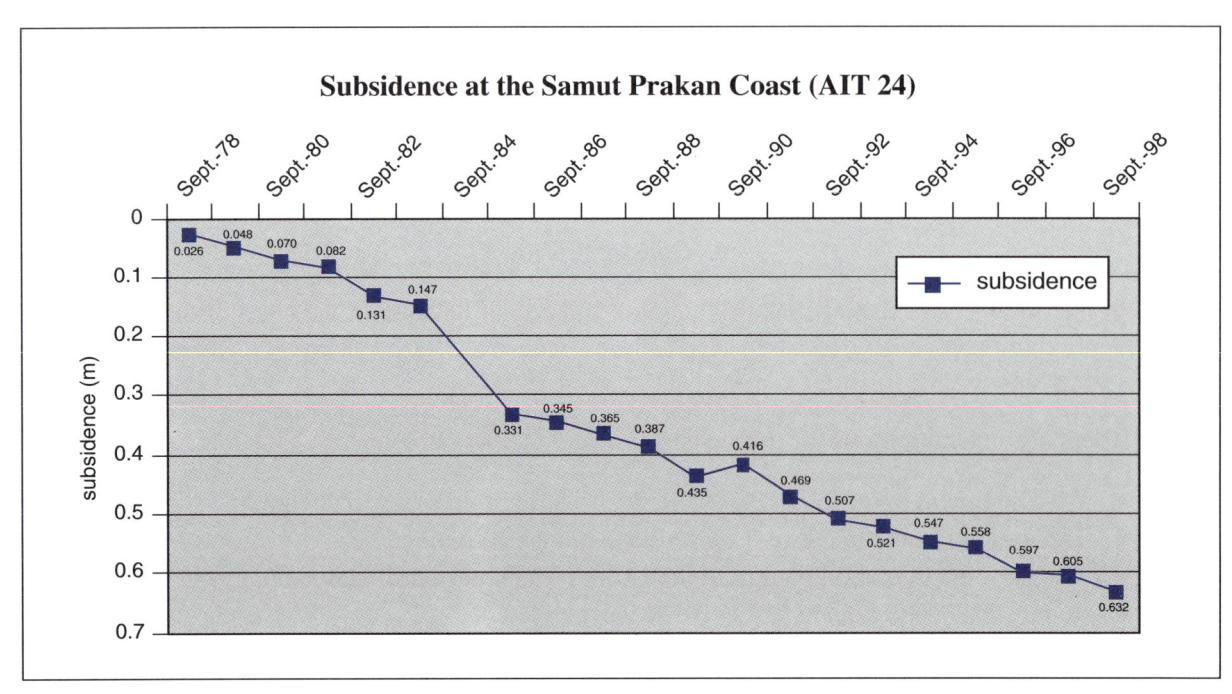

Date	Subsidence (m)
Sept.-78	0.026
	0.048
	0.070
	0.082
Sept.-82	0.131
	0.147
Sept.-84	0.331
	0.345
	0.365
	0.387
Sept.-88	0.435
	0.416
	0.469
	0.507
	0.521
	0.547
	0.558
	0.597
	0.605
Sept.-98	0.632

Figure II.27. Geodetic levellings reveal a lowering of the land of more than 60 cm at AIT benchmark No. 24 (at the coast in Samut Prakan, near the Chao Phraya River mouth between 1978 and 1996)
(See figure II.8 for the exact location of this benchmark)

Figure II.28. Coastal erosion and disappearance of mangrove coast near the mouth of the Ta Chin River, Samut Sakhon Province

a. Mangroves

The coast of the Upper Gulf of Thailand is covered, or rather, was covered, with mangrove forests. Mangrove forests protect the shoreline against wave- and tidal action and erosion. When mangrove forests disappear, the shoreline is unprotected and will erode easily.

Mangrove forests can only be sustainable when sediment availability and sea level are in equilibrium. Young mangroves can only grow when accretion of sediments occurs.

In the Upper Gulf of Thailand a combination of relative rise in sea level (caused by land subsidence as outlined above and the absence of sediments in the coastal waters cause the end of the growth and new development of the mangrove forests.

The other, and probably the most important factor, why the mangrove vegetation is disappearing inland is the cut-down of mangrove trees to create new areas for aquaculture (mainly shrimp farming). Some other factors why the mangrove forest is disappearing, may be pollution of the water, plant diseases and storm surges.

b. Estimation of land subsidence at the coast between Samut Sakhon and the mouth of the Chao Phraya River.

It is difficult to estimate the total land subsidence in this area, because no benchmarks used in this study are located at this part of the coast.

No estimates of groundwater pumpage are available in this part of the Central Plain. However, the use of groundwater by the extensive aquaculture is probably very high. This will lead to a high land subsidence. Since groundwater moves laterally within its aquifer, the groundwater level of the deeper aquifers also decreases far underneath the sea floor, causing land subsidence. Or in this case it would be better to speak of subsidence of the sea floor.

As no measuring results are available it is very difficult to estimate the total land subsidence at the coast, but it is likely that land subsidence is higher than the 2 cm in 2000 as calculated by SURFER. Using the kriging-method of the SURFER software to calculate land subsidence at some parts of the coastline, with the lack of sufficient data, may not be an adequate method.

c. Conclusion

The general conclusion is that the coastal erosion takes places at a rate of several metres per year, but so far precise information is not available. One cause for the coastal erosion is the land subsidence, but also the lesser availability of river sediment and the destruction of the mangrove forest play an important role.

More data on the amount of groundwater pumpage and precise land subsidence data are necessary to understand the relation of land subsidence and the coastal erosion in this specific area.

E. Conclusions and recommendations

1. Conclusions

The land subsidence in Bangkok is an ongoing phenomenon that cannot be easily stopped. Even if groundwater pumping would stop today, the land subsidence will continue for a certain time span.

The causes of the land subsidence in Bangkok are clear, compaction/consolidation of the upper clay layer and overpumping of groundwater, although rate and magnitude of the causes are difficult to calculate.

Land subsidence is a major geological hazard, not only in Bangkok but also throughout the world. It seldom causes fatalities but the annual costs of damages, precautions and remedial works total millions of dollars annually.

It is an insidious geological hazard, rarely hitting the headlines of newspapers. Its diversity and broad range of impacts are suggested as a major cause of the lack of national focus on this hazard in the United States (McCall et al., 1996).

(i)   Land subsidence and groundwater management

A clear relation can be made between land subsidence and groundwater pumping. Implemented measures, such as the Groundwater act of 1983 and the groundwater fee of 1985, have proved to be successful to curb land subsidence in the area. The rate of land subsidence lowered from 5-12 cm per year before 1983 to about 2-4 cm per year in the period 1985-1988.

Also a clear corrrelation can be made between economic prosperity and land subsidence. In times of economic prosperity, groundwater pumping is higher due to increased demand, and thus the land subsidence is higher. After the economic depression in 1997 groundwater pumping decreased.

(ii) Predictions for future land subsidence

On a geological basis it is difficult to predict any land subsidence for the future. The differences in thickness of the clay layer(s) are too small and not known on a detailed scale to designate specific areas where land subsidence will occur in the future.

Some remarks can be made. The results of testing done by Kuecher suggest that the Compression Index is higher with sediments with a finer and more distal facies. For the Bangkok area this may lead to a higher compaction of the Soft Bangkok Clay in the southernmost part of the Central Plain, especially near the coast.

Since land subsidence through overpumping is closely related to industrial development in that area, the land subsidence is expected to be higher where industrial development will be deployed.

Also in areas in the middle of the basin, the groundwater level will remain low for a long timespan, because of lack of natural recharge.

2. Expectations for future consequences

The consequences of the land subsidence as outlined in chapter 4 will continue unless some drastic measures will be taken.

The breakage of sewer systems will continue, causing health problems.

The damage to roads, bridges and buildings will continue costing the government each year millions of bahts in repair costs.

The potential for floods will increase; due to the flooding of rivers, tidal flooding and flooding related to torrential rainfall. Furthermore an expected rise in precipitation by IPCC of about 10-15 per cent for this region could enhance the problem of flooding. These are considerations that need to be taken into account in the urban planning process.

As was shown in some figures under D, the rate of land subsidence is much higher than the rate of sea level rise. Compared with the estimated rise in sea level (4.5 mm per year for the next century, IPCC, 2001) the rate of land subsidence in the Bangkok area will be about ten times higher! Although no predictions were made in this study, it can be postulated that the ongoing exploitation of groundwater can cause land subsidence in coastal areas of around 30-50 mm per year.

Cities such as Shanghai, Manila and Jakarta face familiar threats.

The intrusion of saline water in the Bangkok Aquifer will continue and saline water will eventually also intrude the other aquifers such as Phra Pradaeng, Nakhon Luang and Nontha Buri.

3. Suggestions for action

(i)   Suggested remedial measures

The consequences for the future can be mitigated when adequate measures will be taken. A better planning of groundwater exploitation and a strong decrease of groundwater pumping can lessen this hazard.

Raise the water fee for groundwater use, so that the use of groundwater becomes less attractive over treated surface water.

Extend the area covered by the network of pipelines of the Metropolitan and Provincial Water Authorities (MWA/PWA). Domestic users and industries will use treated surface water instead of pumping of groundwater.

Create retention basins that can accumulate rainwater and flood water. These ponds must be in hydraulic connection with the underlying Bangkok Aquifer. So the use of these ponds is twofold: serve as a retention basin to prevent floodings and recharge fresh water into the saline Bangkok aquifer.

In the Bangkok area many of these pits already exist, at the moment they are in use as sand dredging pits for the construction industry. Only some small-scale adaptations are necessary.

Create small-scale basins connected to the local network of rainwater sewers so that most rainwater can seep into the ground instead of flowing.

Better foundations for roads will be necessary, since the process of compaction of the upper clay layer will always occur where new roads are built. A better foundation can mitigate the damage to the road.

When land subsidence near the coast is not curbed, that area will be more susceptible to coastal erosion and even whole areas shall become flooded when no protective measures (in the form of dikes) will be taken. The construction of dikes and other forms of flood protection will be very expensive. It might be cheaper in the long term to stop the pumping of groundwater now, and replace it with treated surface water.

(ii)   Need for action to come to a better scientific understanding

Some actions that need to be taken to come to a full scientific understanding of the mechanisms, rates and magnitudes of the land subsidence:

- Install some more benchmarks in areas (such as the coast of Samut Prakan and further East) in order to get a good assessment of the rate of land subsidence in those areas.
- Maintain the existing network of benchmarks.

- Some more research on the differences in sedimentary facies (and its matching Compression Index) is necessary to understand more of the spatial variation of compaction of the soft Bangkok Clay layer.
- Other processes such as geochemical changes occurring in clays in relation to saline water intrusion need more study.

References

Asian Institute of Technology (AIT), 1981: Investigation of land subsidence caused by deep well pumping in the Bangkok Area, comprehensive report 1978-1981, 353 p.

Asian Institute of Technology (AIT), 1985: Impact of Quaternary sediments on urban development and land use of the Central Plain of Thailand, AIT research report 224, 175 p.

ESCAP Secretariat, 1988: Geological information for planning in Bangkok, Thailand. In: *ESCAP, Atlas of Urban geology, volume 1*. pp. 24-60.

ESCAP Secretariat, 2000: Integrating Environmental Considerations into the Economic Decision-Making Process, Chapter IV Protection of regional natural environment. Source: *http://www.unescap.org/drpad/pub3/integra/modalities/china/4ch04a.htm*

Intergovernmental Panel on Climate Change (IPCC), 2001: IPCC Workgroup I Third Assessment Report: 'Summary for policymakers' (draft version), source: *http://www.ipcc.ch*

Jarupongsakul, Thanawat, 1999: The implications of sea-level rise and flooding for the gulf of Thailand region. In: *SEAPOL integrated studies of the Gulf of Thailand.*, 1999, pp. 95-157.

Kuecher, G.J., 1995: The dominant processes responsible for subsidence of coastal wetlands in South Lousiana. In: *Land Subsidence, Proc. of the fifth Int. symposium on Land Subsidence.* pp. 69-81.

Nutalaya, P., Rau, J.L., 1981: Bangkok: The sinking metropolis, *Episodes*, Vol. 1981, No. 4.

Phraprasert, Boonchou, 1998: Water demand side management programme for the metropolitan waterworks authority, Thailand. In: *ESCAP: 'towards efficient water use in urban areas in Asia and the Pacific.* pp. 143-146.

Ramnarong, V., Buapeng, S., 1992: Groundwater resources of Bangkok and its vicinity impact and management. In: *Proc. on Geological resources of Thailand: Potential for future development, Bangkok, Thailand.* pp. 172-184.

Rau, J.L., 1994: Urban and environmental issues in East and Southeast Asian coastal lowlands, *Engineering Geology*, 37, pp. 25-29.

Straits Times Interactive, 2000: Planners scramble to save a sinking Bangkok; source: http://www.straitstimes.asia1.com.sg/asia/sea10_0811_prt.html

Yong, R.N., Nutalaya, P., Mohamed, A.M.O. & Xu, D.M., 1991: Land subsidence and flooding in Bangkok. In: *Land subsidence (ed. By A.I. Johnson) (Proc. Fourth Int. Symp. on Land Subsidence, Houston, May 1991) pp.* 407-416, IAHS Publ. No. 200.